Dogs in Action

Dogs in Action

Angela Sayer

Exeter Books

NEW YORK

The author and publishers wish to thank the Guide
Dogs for the Blind Association and the Chief
Constable of Sussex, Sir George Terry CBE, QPM,
for their kind permission to photograph the dogs
and interview their handlers.

Contents

The History of Working
    Breeds 6
Farm and Herding
    Dogs 18
War Dogs, Guard Dogs
    and Police Dogs 34
Draught Dogs 52
Guide Dogs 60
Coursing and Racing
    Dogs 68
Hounds 82
Terriers 94
Gundogs 110
Acknowledgments 128

The History of Working Breeds

There seems little doubt that the dog was the first of all animals to submit itself to domestication by man, and that this unique new association and co-operation allowed man gradually to evolve from a mere hunter into a purposeful herder of flocks. Sharing very similar social systems based on family units, dog and man probably came together as wary hunting partners, each being of benefit to the other by his special skills. Eventually dog and man voluntarily joined forces and the first links were forged in a chain of friendship destined to last through eons of time.

Origin

The precise origin of our domestic dog *Canis familiaris* is the subject of much debate, dispute and speculation even to the present day. The general concenus of opinion, however, is that its ancestors comprise at least three separate and diverse members of the wolf family, which together contain all the genetic information necessary for the evolution of all varieties of our modern dog. A paper published in 1935 by R. I. Pocock cites four families of wolves likely to have formed the basis of the domestic dog's gene pool. They are the Northern Grey Wolf *Canis*

The Northern Grey Wolf, *Canis lupus,* at home in its natural habitat.

lupus, the Pale-footed Asian Wolf *Canis lupus pallipes*, the small Arabian Desert Wolf *Canis lupus arabs* and the Woolly-coated Wolf from Tibet and northern India *Canis lupus laniger*. All wolves and dogs are able to interbreed and produce fertile offspring which helps to confirm their close genetic relationship.

Naturalists Richard and Alice Fiennes carried out further research into the dog's ancestors and somewhat expanded Pocock's views. They suggested that each of four wolf families produced a different group of dogs. From *Canis lupus*, for example, derived such breeds as the Huskies, Samoyeds, Chows, Pomeranians, Elkhounds, Schipperkes, Collies, Alsatians, Corgis and Terriers, while the Dingo group may be traced back to *Canis lupus pallipes*. All the Greyhound group are traced to a long-legged close relative of the Asian Wolf, while today's Mastiffs, Bulldogs, Spaniels, Setters, Pointers, Retrievers and Hounds of all types are said to have come from the Tibetan Wolf, *Canis lupus chanco* or *laniger*. The evidence to support this grouping was gathered from an extensive study of primitive dog remains and their global location, along with the mapping of the migration routes of ancient peoples. The Northern group of dogs are, therefore, considered to have come from northern Europe while the Dingo group almost certainly arose in India. Dogs of the Greyhound group

Wild dogs in the African bush greet each other, exhibiting the same innate behavioural patterns seen in domesticated dogs.

7

were most probably first domesticated in the southern deserts of Persia, while the Mastiff group developed in the mountainous regions from the Himalayas to the Pyrenees.

The Northern group is interesting as it includes sled and sheepdogs but few hunting dogs, the Samoyed and Elkhounds being the exceptions, and like the other Spitz, could well have some pariah blood from the Dingo group. Many zoologists explain the great variation in muzzle length of Northern-group dogs by arguing mixed ancestry, but it must be said that some skull samples of the Northern Wolf also show considerable variation. If skulls of the modern Alsatian and Collie are compared it is quite easy to see how, with selection, these could have evolved from *Canis lupus* as their common ancestor. The Alsatian has existed almost unchanged for about 2000 years, while the Rough Collie is a comparatively modern breed developed for the show ring. Dedicated shepherd dogs such as the Komondor must have originated from crosses between Northern sheepdogs and Mastiffs.

Of the Dingo group, the Australian Dingo is thought to have travelled to Australia from Asia along with the Aborigines about 15 000 years ago. It

Right: The Dingo, wild dog of Australia, was once domesticated, then reverted to a feral form.

Below: A semi-feral dog of pariah type guards an ancient Egyptian temple at Karnak.

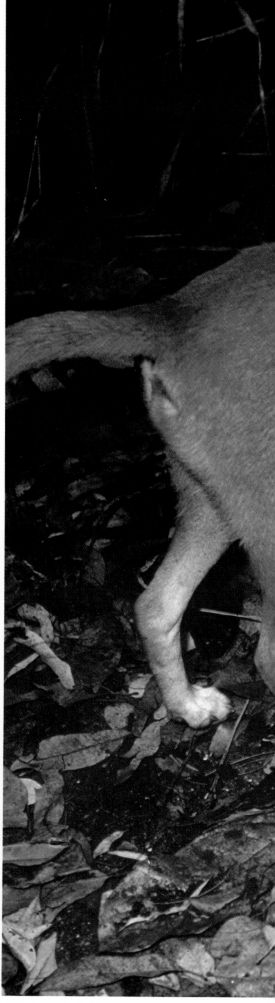

Left: This Pariah dog is similar to a Dingo in colour and conformation. Such dogs roam in scavenging packs in areas of the Far East.

Below: Two dogs of Basenji type at home on an African beach.

was almost certainly domesticated at that time, but eventually returned to a feral mode of life. Very uniform in type, the Dingos of today are able to interbreed with domestic dogs, and puppies taken early from the wild are easily tamed. Pariah dogs also belong to the Dingo group, but differ from the true Dingo in having curled up tails. The Basenji is an African dog of this group, an ancient breed, and very similar to small dogs shown in Ancient Egyptian art. Today's Greyhounds and Salukis are also similar to those of the Pharaohs, and dogs of Mastiff type have always shown themselves to be invaluable in the service of man.

Domestication, Diversification and Specialization

Whatever the true origins of the domestic dog we do have fossil evidence of early domestication from Paleolithic remains discovered in Russia. Along with human remains, bones of a new extinct type of dog, *Canis pontiatini*, were found and imply that domestication could have commenced in this area between 10 000 and 7000 years ago.

At this time man was very wasteful in his hunting habits and often ran large herds of herbivores over steep cliffs, eating what meat he and his nomadic tribe could manage, and leaving

This Egyptian relief of the XVIII Dynasty shows an efficient dog of mastiff type hunting ostriches. Cairo Museum.

the rest for other predators and scavengers. Such practices would soon have been exploited by wolves and jackals, and it is more than likely that the boldest animals became camp-followers, certain of some meat at the end of each hunt. Before long, a form of co-operation is likely to have evolved, man pack and wolf pack working in unison to effect the kills. Over a very long period of time the man and wolf relationship must have strengthened. Maybe an orphaned cub was taken into the camp to be hand reared, or maybe the wolves, jackals or primitive dogs were attracted closer and closer to the camps by discarded scraps of food.

However the first bonds were made, it is apparent that dog and man were already close friends in Denmark between 8000 and 6000 years ago. In Mesolithic settlements excavated there, bones of two different types of domesticated dog were discovered and are generally referred to as the Maglemose dogs.

Other well-documented remains of the early domesticated dog were found in the lake settlements of Switzerland. Dated at approximately 4000 B.C., again there were two quite distinct types. One, called the 'Lake Dog', closely resembled the primitive Russian remains and the front part of this animal was proportionately better developed than its hind parts. The jaw was extremely strong, and the bite must have been particularly powerful. It is thought that this was a hunting dog, ideal for holding quite large prey, and that it is a likely ancestor of the Spitz group of modern dogs. The second type is known as the 'Peat Dog' and had a rounded head, shorter muzzle and a moderately strong jaw. Experts tend to agree that this animal was probably used for herding rather than for hunting and is likely to have been an ancestor of the modern Pinschers, Schnauzers and Terriers.

Excavations in Egypt have yielded valuable early evidence of domesticated dogs. The Ancient Egyptians had several quite distinct types of dog, obviously developed to perform specific functions. One bas-relief found in Thebes, dated around 1450 B.C., shows pictures of Saluki-type hounds pulling down game. Hunting in the desert required the use of very fast 'sight' hounds, and for this the Saluki would have proved ideal. In the tomb of Tutankhamun, an interesting find was the ornate ostrich feather fan dec-

orated with a scene around its gold base, showing the boy-king in his chariot and armed with a bow, hunting ostriches pursued by a speeding Saluki.

Dogs were worshipped in Ancient Egypt and deeply mourned at death, being carried in ceremony to the embalmers amidst much wailing and beating of gongs. The owner of a dead dog would shave off his own eyebrows

Below: Wild Timber Wolves surround the carcase of their prey, a mule deer.

Bottom: Dogs of the Spitz group have typically fox-like muzzles and tails carried in a curve over their backs.

Above: A huge Mastiff clearly depicted on an Assyrian wall relief of 640 B.C. British Museum, London.

Left: A hound accompanies the hunting chariot on this bas relief from Malatya, now in the Ankara Museum.

Above: Hounds of the Assyrian King Assurbanipal (669–626 B.C.) hunting wild asses. British Museum, London.

Below: A fine basalt statue of the Ptolemaic period represents a sturdy, mastiff-like dog. Musée du Louvre, Paris.

as a sign of grief and mourning, and spare no expense in the embalming and burial rites. Mummified dogs of the period are often well preserved and still complete with elaborate collars bearing their pet names such as 'Ebony' and 'Grabber'. Pictures of dogs in life are seen in tomb paintings and in carved relief on many temple walls. There are Terrier-types, Pointers, Mastiffs, Salukis and a dog that closely resembles the breed now called the Pharaoh Hound. Dogs are shown with both pricked and pendant ears, straight and curled tails, long and short legs, and with plain and patterned coats. The heavier Mastiff-types are generally depicted as battle dogs, while the longer-legged finer dogs are seen helping in hunting scenes. On one tomb dated at 2700 B.C. dogs of the Spitz type are clearly shown while scenes of 2000 B.C. show dogs very similar indeed to our modern Greyhound, but with bushy and slightly curled tails. From 2000–800 B.C. there is evidence of an increase in the diversity of canine types, and it is obvious that some kind of selective breeding was encouraged.

During the successive civilizations of Sumeria, Babylon and Assyria we learn of dogs used for various purposes, mainly for hunting, retrieving game from water, and digging up quarry that had gone to ground. Some fire-blackened reliefs, now in the British Museum, were discovered during excavations of the palace of Assyrian King Assurbanipal who lived from 669–626 B.C. On one panel, two ferocious Mastiffs may be seen straining against their strong leashes, while on another panel, they are shown in the hunt, pulling down onagers and lions. The Babylonians were quite ruthless and cruel in battle, and bred fierce dogs of war.

The Israelites, one-time captives of the Assyrians, despised most animals, particularly the dog. Biblical references include such passages as 'Him that dieth in the streets shall the dogs eat', 'Ye shall not eat any flesh that is torn of the beasts in the field, ye shall cast it to the dogs', and 'Give that which is not holy unto the dogs'. Job made it clear that he considered it the duty of dogs to guard the flocks in the fields.

The Ancient Greeks considered dogs invaluable for hunting purposes and also used them in battle. They developed one huge breed in the town of Mollossus, and these Mollossian dogs were renowned both as guards and shepherders. At Epidaurus and in the temples of Athens, healing dogs were kept especially to treat wounded or injured persons. They did this by licking the afflicted areas with their wet tongues. The efficacy of this practice is recorded on a stone tablet which reads, 'Thyson of Hermione is blind of both eyes; a temple dog licks the organs and he immediately regains his sight.' Dogs feature greatly in Ancient Greek art, and it is obvious that the *Melitaeus* or Maltese dog was kept as a pet and valued for its heavy coat and diminutive size.

Below: Hunting dogs are clearly shown on the interior panel of the Gundestrup Bowl discovered in a Danish peat-bog and dated about 200 B.C.

Above: This plate, a scene from pagan Celtic Britain, establishes the fact that the dog had become the companion of contemporary man.

The Romans also valued dogs, especially the larger types, using them in battle and as guards. Roman dogs became victims too, however, for the ascent of Sirius, the dog-star, was accompanied by sweltering August weather. This period was known as the dog-days, and unfortunate pet dogs were sacrificed so that precious crops would be protected from the intense heat.

The oldest known British dog was discovered as an intact skeleton in 1928, during the excavation of the now-famous Windmill Hill site in Wiltshire. At the top of a gently rounded hill just outside the town of Avebury, three concentric lines of earthworks were found and dated at 2500 B.C. This area was inhabited by Neolithic Stone Age men who had arrived from Europe to colonize southern England around 3000 B.C. As such men changed from nomadic hunting habits to those of settled farmers, new demands were placed on the dogs that lived with them. Rather than chasing, holding and killing other animals for food and hides, dogs now had a new role and were expected to guard small flocks and herds against attack from wild beasts and other marauding men.

The Windmill Hill dog was remarkably well preserved and closely resembled the Lake Dog of Switzerland, but there was nothing with the remains to indicate the animal's exact function in the ancient settlement. Other British excavations at the fortress of Maiden Castle, Dorset, showed evidence that dogs were associated with human burial rites, between 100–50 B.C., and two distinct types of dog were apparent, both of which were larger than the Windmill Hill dog. One type was obviously of the Spitz group, while the second was larger and of a Mastiff type probably brought to Britain around 500 B.C. by the Celts or perhaps by Phoenician sea traders.

As the great trade routes spread across the continents and intrepid sailors crossed the hostile seas, the dog family

A fine mosaic showing a Roman hunting scene. 2nd century A.D.

Left: In Pisanello's *Vision of St. Eustace* some fine greyhounds are shown, with spaniels and more mastiffs. National Gallery, London.

spread and multiplied, each area developing its own types to serve particular purposes. In wide open arid regions 'sight' hounds were considered best for running down game, while in wooded or undulating country, 'scent' hounds were needed. Large fearless dogs were necessary to guard property and animals, and dogs with natural herding ability were able to keep flocks and herds under control.

In the golden age of Hywel Dda, the good and kindly Welsh king passed strict laws covering a variety of matters, including a set of codes relating to dogs. These were clearly differentiated thus: 'There are three higher kinds of dog – the dog which hunts by sight, the greyhound and the spaniel. There are three kinds of dog which hunt by scent – the bloodhound, the covert hound and the harrier. There are three kinds of curs, the mastiff, the shepherd dog and the house dog.' There were strict fines for the killing of a dog. This was known as its blood-price, and the value of a dog was proportionate to the rank of its master. A covert hound belonging to the King was valued at one pound, while a similar dog belonging to a noble was worth only half that price, and that owned by a peasant worth only four pence, then one-sixtieth part of the pound. Very high fines were also levied for injuries inflicted on any of the King's prized hunting hounds.

The bloodprice of a shepherd dog was determined by its abilities, and the most valuable dog of this type was

expected to be able to lead out the cattle early in the morning, to drive them home at night and to maintain a night watch, patrolling the herd at least three times during the hours of darkness. Dogs which attacked people were given warnings, and after four reported attacks had to be destroyed. If any owner refused to comply with this law, he would be tied tightly to his dog, while the unfortunate animal was stoned to death in the public market place.

In other parts of Europe at about the same time, a sheepdog commanded a high price if it was able to attack a wolf, rescue a lamb from its jaws and give the alarm to neighbouring farms.

As civilizations developed man learned to improve his dogs, increasing their skills at their respective tasks by careful selection of breeding stock. Man soon learned to appreciate beauty of form as well as skill in work, and pride of ownership gradually emerged. The adaptive dog soon filled every niche available to it in the

lives of man and his family and since the first days of its domestication has proved to be a loyal and trustworthy servant.

The work of many dogs has changed and been adapted over the centuries. No longer do fine ladies need their lap dogs or comforters to attract fleas and lice from infesting their own bodies, and the need for the Turnspit or kitchen dogs to rotate the meat slowly roasting over the open fire has also disappeared. The use of dogs as pack and draught animals has been discontinued in most countries and indeed has been made illegal in many. Few civilized men now enjoy the spectacle of watching dogs fighting one another or being used to bait other unfortunate animals, but despite the general worldwide change in attitudes many dogs still fulfill very necessary functions as working animals.

Lap dogs and pillow dogs became common in medieval times, and were used to attract fleas from their owners' bodies to their own. Victoria and Albert Museum, London.

Above: Dogs of mastiff type also appear in the treatise on hunting by Gaston Phebus, Comte de Foix, 1382. British Museum, London.

Farm and Herding Dogs

The first true dog book to be published in Britain was designed as a treatise on hunting and was called the *Boke of St. Albans*, written by Dame Juiliana Berners in 1486. Prioress of Sopwell Nunnery in St. Albans, the authoress was an ardent sportswoman, enthralled with the thrill of the chase and all matters related to every sort of hunting. As might be expected, the

An early Spanish picture showing a shepherd rewarding his hard-working herding dog with fresh milk.

dogs referred to in her work are mainly sporting breeds and her lists of races reads 'Fyrste there is a Greyhoun, a Bastard, a Mongrell, a Mastiff, a Lemor, a Spanyel, Raches, Kenetts, Teroures, Butcher's Hounds, Myddng dogges, Tryndeltaylles, and Prikherid currys, and smalle ladyes' poppees that bere awaye the flees.' It is not easy to recognize all of the breeds that the Prioress names, written in 1605, but Shakespeare's *King Lear* gives a clearer list:

'Mastiff, greyhound, mongrel grim
Hound or Spaniel, brach or lym,
Or bobtail tike or trundle-tail.'

It would seem, therefore, that the Tryndeltaylle or trundle-tail was likely to have been a working sheepdog, and possibly the ancestor of today's working Collies.

In 1570 another author, Dr. Johannes Caius, chief physician to Queen Elizabeth I, wrote a Latin paper all about the British dogs of his time and, six years later, the work was translated into English and published by Abraham Fleming. The fourth section of the book is concerned with farm dogs and describes '*Canis pastoralis*, the Shepherd's Dogge which hath sundry names derived from sundry circumstances'. In the 18th century Buffon drew up an evolutionary tree in which he attempted to show the genealogy of all dog breeds known at that time. All of the dogs discussed were shown as having descended from the Shepherd Dog, and Buffon's theory was strongly supported by all the written material available at that time. Linnaeus, too, at about the same time, compiled his own classification of animals and has the Sheepdog appearing second in a long list of dog breeds and designated *Canis Domesticus* or Shepherd's Dog.

Published in 1791, the Dublin edition of the *Encyclopaedia Britannica* has domestic dogs arranged into five main classes, one of which is clearly the Sheepdog group. A contemporary plate shows an example of the Shepherd Dog, which is very similar to the working Collie of today. When the licensing of dogs became law in 1796, sheepdogs and cattle dogs were normally exempted if owned by poor people, and in any case subject to reduced license fees.

Pastoral Breeds Today

Today's farm and pastoral dogs show considerable variation in type and general appearance, for although they may perform similar tasks, the areas where they were developed for work are also very variable in climate and terrain. Most pastoral dogs are true sheepdogs and have equally efficient powers of sight, scent and hearing. This family of dogs also shows a conformity of head shape, with plenty of width and brain room across the dome and a well-formed and powerful muzzle. Most sheepdogs' tails are often left at their natural length and are carried low, curling up slightly at the tip. A few breeds have tails curled in the Spitz fashion and some breeds, particularly those used as cattle dogs, have their tails docked short. Sheepdogs vary considerably in size, ranging from the diminutive **Shetland Sheepdog** which may be only 12 inches (30 cm) at the shoulder to the **Russian Owtzharka** which sometimes attains a height of 32 inches (81 cm). Coat type varies too, and dogs from cold regions naturally develop thick woolly coats, while those in temperature zones have soft thin coats of fine hair. Some sheepdogs, like the **Komondor** and **Puli** from Hungary, have coats formed from thick matted cords of hair, which in their natural habitat help them to work efficiently, with their true canine shape quite disguised, among the native flocks of semi-wild sheep. The Komondor is large and white and merges well with the prairie flocks, while the much smaller and dark-coated Puli works mainly on the edge of the plains, its wandering independent habit often curbed by being tethered to iron hoops or logs.

The terrain is an important factor in determining the best sort of dog to be used for shepherding, but the farmer's choice may also depend on the local predators. In areas of Turkey, for example, where wolves are still prevalent, the sheepdog must also act as a fearless guard, and to this end a strong dog rather like a scaled-down St. Bernard has been developed. In Mexico the big Merino sheep like to stay in tightly grouped flocks and are, therefore, comparatively easy to muster

In this early work the mounted falconers are accompanied by a leashed greyhound and a pack of heavier hounds of the Talbot type.

Top: Working collies keep a vigilant watch for trouble.

Above: This unusual dog is a Caucasian sheepdog at work in the U.S.S.R.

Right: The Komondor is a Hungarian sheepdog, noted for its unusual corded coat.

Left: During an Australian dog-training course 'Mark' the Alsatian is encouraged to bottle-feed a lamb.

Right: The Kelpie is a keen Australian shepherding dog, an intelligent, efficient breed.

Australian Cattle Dogs generally work in pairs as 'heelers' to control their often wayward charges.

However the dogs that herd them are expected to perform dual roles and protect their charges from predators at night. The **German Shepherd Dog**, or **Alsatian**, is a very capable and versatile breed and one of the oldest of the shepherding dogs. Its high level of intelligence has enabled it to be used in its native land for a unique form of herding, that is trotting to and fro forming an invisible fence to enable flocks to economically strip-graze sectors of pasture land. Perhaps the most specialized of all the sheepdogs, however, is the **Huntaway** of New Zealand which is specially bred and trained to deal with the rough, high ground of that country's South Island. Although the upper grazing limits are determined by the snow-line, the sheep tend to panic and run downhill if they are unduly disturbed. It is the Huntaway's job to keep active and barking to ensure that the sheep stay up on the hill. In Australia sheepdogs have devloped the technique of 'backing' which entails running on the backs of tightly bunched sheep, moving them in the desired direction by barking at the leaders. The **Kelpie** is perhaps the best known of the working dogs of Australia. It was developed from the old Scottish and Welsh sheepdogs taken to their new country by early settlers, and the foundation bitch was a cross between a Dingo and a working Collie called 'Caesar'. Extraordinarily sensitive and very conscientious in its work, one Kelpie can manage a huge flock of sheep, either on the open range or moving to new pasture. A perfect product of its environment, the Australian Kelpie is about 19 inches high and has a short, harsh and hard-wearing coat. Since its creation in 1875, it has developed into a fine utilitarian and standardized breed.

The **Heeler**, or the **Australian Cattle Dog**, is another good worker and is said to have been bred down from early Scottish blue-merle Collies, spiced with a dash of Dingo blood, just like the Kelpie. It is a very agile, mobile dog and works entirely with cattle which it drives and controls by nipping at their heels, hence its descriptive name.

Another 'heeler' is the **Welsh Corgi**, bred in two distinct varieties, the Cardigan which is the most popular for working, and the Pembroke which is now considered more suitable as a house pet and show dog. Both varieties share a common origin, and the name is said to have derived from 'cor' meaning 'dwarf' and 'ci' meaning 'dog' although a dictionary of the Welsh Language published in 1859 states that the correct translation is 'cur dog'. The word. 'cur', now has a derogatory meaning when applied to the dog, and *The Oxford English Dictionary's* definition of the word as a 'worthless, low-bred or snappish dog' is modern and far from correct. The Ancient Welsh Laws, codified by Hywel Dda around the year 920, make frequent references to curs. One statement lists three items indispensable to a summer resident: 'a bothy [hut]; a herdman's cur; and a knife'. In a further section, cur was used to describe a whole group of dogs including a watch cur, a shepherd cur and a house cur. Furthermore, the bloodprice of a herdsman's cur was said to equal that of an ox, and was, therefore, worth more than one of the King's fine Buckhound pups. Curs were taken by Welsh families who settled in the southern and western States of America, and were invaluable in herding cattle and sheep as well as proving themselves fine hunters of wild pigs and waterfowl for the cooking pot. Unfortunately the Cur, as a distinct type, became extinct in America *circa* 1870.

The brave little Welsh Corgi prospered, however, earning its keep over the years. In the 15th century such dogs were used to move herds of black Welsh cattle eastwards to market. The stock of many small farmers was gathered together and farriers were employed to fit iron shoes to the cloven hooves of all the cattle; then teams of drovers started out with their charges on the long hard journey to London's Smithfield Market. Travelling had to be slow, so that the cattle could feed and also have time to ruminate, thoroughly digesting each meal, and the dogs were always busy, keeping the cattle together to prevent any

straying. On narrow stretches of road, the dogs had to keep the herd bunched and under control to allow the passage of other travellers and the occasional stagecoach. Many drovers were, in effect, government agents and often carried large sums of money for the payment of taxes and other debts, and the herds and their keepers were sometimes menaced by highwaymen. In 1735 Tom King and Dick Turpin, two of the most notorious 'gentlemen of the road', teamed up especially to rob the Welsh drovers as they approached the end of their long journey. Turpin was born in the small village of Newport in Essex, and as a young man started

[Torchlight View of Smithfield.]

Above: London's Smithfield market, a place where cattle dogs such as the Welsh Corgi were employed as early as the 15th century.

Left: Derived from 'cor' meaning 'dwarf' and 'gi' meaning 'dog' this Welsh breed has been an invaluable worker for several centuries.

Left: Cattle were driven to market over long stretches of often dangerous terrain and dogs acted as both drovers and guards.

Below: Once known as the Smithfield, the Old English Sheepdog is still used for working stock on some farms.

work as a butcher, but soon abandoned honest labour for the excitement and quick rewards of highway robbery. Turpin, King and their Essex gang robbed the drovers of cattle as well as their money but had to fight off the furious and fearless cattle dogs which would attack the footpads on sight. The dogs were often seriously wounded in such encounters and were then left to recover in nearby inns or taverns to be collected on the drovers' return journey. Having safely sold their cattle, the drovers were able to return to Wales by safer routes, carrying cash back to their employers. Their arduous and dangerous job was very well paid and a few of the Welshmen earned sufficient money to allow early retirement. It is recorded that five ex-drovers subscribed with Dr. Samuel Johnson towards the publishing of *Gorchestion Beirdd Cymru*, the Golden Treasury of Wales. With such men as their masters and such an admirable history it is little wonder that the Welsh Corgi remains so popular today, even enjoying life as the pampered pet of the British Royal household.

The Swedish **Vallhund** is very similar to the Corgi in both conformation and temperament, and almost certainly stems from a common ancestor. It is primarily used for working cattle, although it is also good with sheep, and has remained of fixed type for many years.

Another breed developed for droving work is the **Old English Sheepdog**, originally known as the Smithfield or Cotswold Sheepdog, and

used through the 17th and 18th centuries for taking cattle, sheep and ponies from the New Forest of Hampshire to Smithfield market in London. In Dr. Gordon Stables' book, *Our Friend the Dog*, published almost one hundred years ago, he describes the drover's dog. 'This is a shaggy-coated, hard-haired, hard-headed rough-and-right sort of a dog without much of a tail, very often to be seen accompanying the drovers of the Southern Counties. I have seen some of them, not pretty only, but particularly beautiful, and seemingly possessed of a high degree of intelligence. I dare say if they were as much admired as the Highland Collie they would become refined in their manners, but refinement is not a strong point with the Bob-Tailed Collie, any more than it is with his master. The colour is usually black and tan or steel grey. I like the latter very much; I don't know why but it strikes me as being a hardier colour.' Today the lovable Bobtail is primarily a show dog and is only rarely worked; its profuse

coat, bred in to withstand all the vagaries of the British climate, is now shampooed and conditioned to such an extent that the Bobtail is in great demand as a photographic fashion and advertising model. Although the breed cannot be accurately traced back for more than 200 years, it is very similar to other ancient breeds like the **Chien Berger de Brie**, or **Briard**.

The Briard possesses written breed records dating back to the 12th century and Charlemagne is said to have given breeding pairs of these dogs as presents to his closest friends. The Emperor Napoleon was fond of the breed and took several such dogs with him on his expedition to Egypt where they interbred with local sheepdogs and helped to establish the **Armant**, or native **Egyptian Sheepdog**. The Briard is found all over France and is an excellent guard dog as well as herder. During the First World War, both French and American troops were impressed by the breed, and by 1920 breeding stock had been imported into the United States. The British took

Above: The Briard or Chien Berger de Brie has breed records dating back to the 12th century.

Right: Most sheepdogs are faithful, devoted companions and here 'Boy' takes charge of his master's pony.

longer to appreciate the Briard, but by 1974 they had become well enough established to merit the awarding of Challenge Certificates in British shows.

Most countries of the world have their own specialized breeds of Sheepdog and perhaps the best known of all is the working **Collie**. The word 'collie' is interesting in itself. 'Col' is an old Anglo-Saxon word meaning 'black' and was used by Shakespeare in his *Midsummer Night's Dream* to describe the blackness of night:

'Swift as a shadow, short as any dream,
Brief as the lightening in the collied night.'

The ancestors of the famous black-faced sheep of the Scottish Highlands were first called coll-faced or coll-headed sheep; then the term was shortened, for convenience, to colley. Agile and very timid, the flocks of colleys were difficult to manage over the mountain terrain, and gradually an efficient race of intelligent sheepdogs was developed to cope with them, and were quite naturally known as 'Colley Dogs'. Although the names Scotch Colley and Colley Dog have now become obsolete, today's working Collie breeds still retain most of the attributes of their old namesakes.

Ability is more important than looks in a working sheepdog and such dogs have been bred for centuries from tried and tested parents. Many of the most efficient and easily trained strains are inbred, prized by their owners and handlers, and coveted by overseas farmers.

Perhaps best known of all the working sheepdogs is the **Border Collie**, a comparatively new name for a type of dog bred for hundreds of years, and originally known as 'creepers' or 'strong-eyed dogs' in Scotland, land of their birth. The difference between the Border Collie and other types of working sheepdog is in its unique style of working using its 'strong-eye' to fix the sheep and make them do exactly as it wishes. The Border Collie is very submissive to its handler and has almost over-developed herding instincts. For example, puppies of this type will naturally gather together hens and other small creatures. These traits make this dog ideal for obedience and trials work as well as an invaluable aid for working with very large flocks of sheep.

Right: The shepherd relies heavily on the skills of his dog when bad weather is experienced at lambing time.

Sheepdog Trials

In 1837 the Reverend E. B. Wallace, writing about Scottish agriculture and its systems, said 'One important improvement in our agriculture exists in the cultivation and training of a good breed of sheepdog. The same work in gathering and separating flocks of sheep can be more effectively done and with less injury to the sheep, by one man and a good dog, than by the forty or fifty men formerly assembled for these activities. . . .' These remarks hold true today and Sheep Dog Trials are held to test the performance of dogs in carrying out precisely the same tasks that comprise their normal daily work.

The first ever Sheep Dog Trial was held at Bala in North Wales in 1873. Ten dogs competed and the winner, though resident in Wales, was a Scotsman, with his Scottish-bred dog. From that day trials have increased in popularity and were helped by the formation of the International Sheep Dog Society in 1906.

Since 1920 the Society has staged both National and International Trials culminating in the award of Supreme Champion. Today popular media coverage of such trials has increased public awareness of the working sheepdog. In Great Britain viewers

Below right: In the Pyrenees the sheepdog must be able to seek out lost or straying sheep, often working out of range of the shepherd's whistle.

Below: Here four collies give a fine display of controlling sheep.

of the television series *One Man and His Dog* have been enthralled by the obvious skills of the shepherds and the responses of the dogs in carrying out the often demanding trial runs. The programme presenters have taken care to explain just what motivates the dogs to work as they do and why sheep act in their own inimitable manner in response to the dogs.

Training Sheepdogs

Despite years of domestication, sheep still retain an inborn fear of attack by predators, and for this reason they not only bunch together but respond to possible threats by exhibiting set patterns of behaviour. It is because of this that it has been possible to train dogs to control these very important producers of wool and meat.

Just as the sheep have retained the instinctive responses of their wild and ancient ancestors, the sheepdog has retained hunting and pack instincts from his own forebears. By careful selective breeding man has strengthened the hunting instinct in the sheepdog to such an extent that it cannot prevent itself from wanting to run out and

Right: Early training being given by a shepherd to his two young Border Collie pups.

Far right: 'Kim', a working collie, easily clears a hurdle barricade as he helps to round up sheep at shearing time.

around the sheep, and to get down on its belly in order stealthily to stalk them. What *has* changed is the fact that the dog will not attack or kill the sheep. It has been conditioned to submit so fully to its handler, whom it considers its pack leader, that the killing instinct is always under complete control.

Whether training a dog to work sheep generally or to progress to the polished trials standard, the shepherd starts in precisely the same way. Puppies are bred from carefully selected parents, and any one that is to be run and trained is brought up normally, fed on a good balanced diet and watched very carefully. Sheepdog puppies have an inborn herding instinct which has evolved from the hunting instinct and the shepherd must wait patiently until he sees the puppy start to 'run'. This vital change in the pup's behaviour usually starts at about six to nine months of age, or it may not happen until the dog is a year or more, but until this natural instinct manifests itself, it is impossible to train the dog to work sheep. The shepherd may teach the young dog to lie down when told, but give little other training. He watches it carefully, noting its behaviour towards sheep. Finally, one day, without warning, the dog will 'run', taking off and running out after the stock; then its training must immediately begin. Some puppies run out and right around the flock the very first time, while in others the hunting instinct is so strong that they run into

the crowd of sheep and grab one by its flank. This is corrected by the shepherd so that the young dog realizes its mistake, but it must not be so severely punished that it is frightened to approach the sheep closely in the future. Although the herding instinct is strong, sheepdogs are able to be controlled because their submissive instinct which forces each animal to obey its pack leader, the role adopted by the shepherd, is even stronger. The puppy is trained slowly and carefully, learning each stage thoroughly before being taken on to the next. The young dog is never allowed to lose its concentration or become so tired that it lacks eagerness in its work.

During the first six or seven months of its training, the sheepdog is taught to come, sit, stay and walk to heel in practically the same way as other types of dog. It is also taught to accept being chained or tethered in the farm yard without fretting or whining. To work with sheep the dog also has to learn to respond to commands to go left or right and backwards or forwards, as well as to drop down without question. Most trainers teach these actions when the young dog is actually working with sheep. Great emphasis is placed on the close proximity with sheep throughout the puppy's initiation process and some shepherds keep a few sheep near the puppy when it is tethered in the yard.

The sheepdog's eagerness to move sheep must be preserved at all times, but flock training cannot be com-

menced in earnest until the young dog is sufficiently developed to run as fast as the sheep. Flock training starts by loosing the young dog and letting it chase a single sheep back to the flock. Sheep with good herding tendencies are used with a young dog so that it is less likely to make early mistakes. The trainer watches carefully to note his student's natural abilities and failings, and when the dog has become used to the sight and smell of the sheep, training begins in earnest. The dog is taught to cast in an arc behind the sheep, then to bring them towards the trainer; then it learns to head the sheep from in front. Signals are given by whistle and by arm movements at this stage, and gradually the sheepdog is able to distinguish and respond to about 30 different commands. When a young dog begins to move the sheep with confidence, it will be taught to work with other dogs and with larger flocks, and will understand that it must only respond to its own set of signals and commands.

Working sheepdogs are able to take complete control of very large flocks, and in severe winter weather have saved the lives of countless stranded and floundering sheep in deep snow drifts. Even today there is nothing that can possibly replace the unique partnership of the shepherd and his dog.

Overleaf: A champion New Zealand 'eye dog' controlling an aggressive ram by staring him directly in the eyes to gain dominance.

War Dogs, Guard Dogs and Police Dogs

Ancestry and Development of the Dogs of War

The first dogs of war were huge Mastiff-like animals with heavily wrinkled heads and curled tails. Such dogs appear, marching with the armies of Hammurabi, King of Babylon, on bas-reliefs of almost 4000 years ago. More closely resembling today's **Mastiff** is the dog featured on tablets taken from the palace of Assurbanipal, who lived from 669–626 B.C. Here the dogs are taking part in hunting scenes rather than being employed as dogs of war. These great dogs were probably descendants of the Simocyon Dog of the Miocene period which is thought to have evolved in two separate streams, the larger of which, *Simocyon*

diaphorus, is believed to have given rise to dogs such as the great Tibetan Mastiff, and 'in turn' to breeds like the Pyrenean and Bernese Mountain Dogs and the St. Bernard.

Babylon was a city of dog-lovers and terra-cotta plaques depicting Mastiff-like dogs have been found, buried under the thresholds of dwelling houses, presumably as a charm against thieves or evil spirits. From Babylon, the Mastiff spread to Ancient Egypt and, in 485 B.C., Xerxes, King of Persia, brought his great war dogs into Greece. Not only did these animals take important roles in many battles, they also helped to guard the mountain flocks in Ancient Epirus and Sparta. These great dogs were known

A Greek fresco, 1300 B.C., showing domesticated mastiff-like hounds in pursuit of a wild boar. Archaeological Museum, Athens.

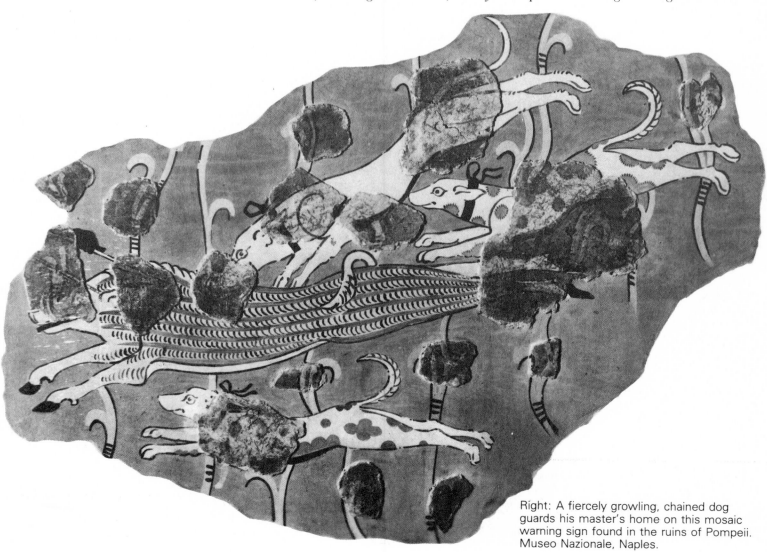

Right: A fiercely growling, chained dog guards his master's home on this mosaic warning sign found in the ruins of Pompeii. Museo Nazionale, Naples.

Early bloodhounds being encouraged to follow a scent trail.

Preceding page: A pair of magnificent English Mastiffs.

as the Mollossi and were prized for their fierce fighting abilities. The Phoenicians probably carried such dogs as trade goods to Old Dalmatia from Greece and Syria, and as the animals settled in each new area, selective breeding resulted in the development of distinctive types.

When the Romans invaded Britain in 54 B.C., they were astonished to find great ferocious dogs fighting alongside their masters, and reported the fact back to Rome. Eventually an officer known as the Procurator Cynegli was appointed and his duties were to collect suitable dogs and to ship them back to Rome where they were used in the arena, and pitted against bears, bulls, lions and tigers.

Later in history, dogs of Mastiff-type were used as guards, and feature in the Forest Laws of King Canute,

which are headed: 'Carta de Foresta of King Canutus, a Dane and a King of this Realme, granted at Parliament holden at Winchester in the year of our Lord 1016.'

The law pertaining to Mastiffs was designed to prevent them catching deer or other game in the strictly preserved forest areas, and ruled that the dogs should be disabled by a mutilating operation known as expedition. The law gave strict instructions for the operation: 'Three claws of the forefoot shall be cut off by the skin; and accordingly, the same is now bled, for the mastives being brought to set one of his forefeet upon a piece of wood eight inches thicke, and a foot square, the one with a mallet, setting a chissell of two inches broad upon the three claws of his forefoot at one blow doth smite them cleane off, and this is the manner

persons within the forest confines, for keeping a Mastiff that had not been 'lawed', while a decree made during the reign of Henry VII protected from expeditation, the Mastiffs of the Abbot of Beaulieu in the New Forest. Such excused dogs were known as Ban-dogs or Band-dogs, and had to be kept chained up during the day, unless they were muzzled. For diversions, many band-dogs were used for the baiting of bulls, bears and other animals, and were said to be quite fearless. In Shakespeare's *King Henry V* are the lines: 'That island of England breeds very valiant creatures, their mastiffs are of unmatchable courage.'

Mastiffs fought with their masters at the Battle of Agincourt in 1415 and as Sir Piers Leigh of Lyme Park lay mortally wounded, his Mastiff bitch stayed by his side, fiercely guarding his body. The Lyme Park Mastiffs were bred for four or five centuries in unbroken lines of descent, at their home in Stockport, Cheshire, and were the forebears of today's Old English Mastiffs. James I gave some Lyme Mastiffs to Phillip III of Spain and it is possible that the large dog in *Las Meninas* painted by Velezquez is one of their descendants. In Mexico and the West Indies, the Spanish armies used their Mastiffs to hunt down the Indians.

During the reign of King Henry VIII, a poet was created for a Master of the King's Bears, Bulls and Mastiffs, a position which was to endure until 1642. King Henry placed great value on his Mastiffs and sent 400 of the fighting dogs to Charles V of Spain, who used them in his war with Francis I of France. These Mastiffs were extremely fierce and unpredictable, and were invaluable in warning of ambushes or the approach of enemy forces. In 1540, an envoy of Henry VII wrote home from France: 'The Constable took me to the King's Dinner whom we found speaking of certain masties you gave him at Calais, and how long it took to train them, for when he first let slip one at a wild boar, he spied a white horse with a page upon him and he took the horse by the throat and they could not pluck him off until he had strangled it. He laughed very heartily while telling this. . . .'

Baiting sports were extremely popular for several centuries and although bulls and bears were the usual unfortunate victims, sometimes lions or even horses were used for public

King Philip IV of Spain, shown in hunting attire in the painting by Velazquez, and accompanied by a large hound of mastiff descent. Museo del Prado, Madrid.

of expeditating mastives.' Although this cruel practice was first designed to prevent poaching, it later became a means of collecting revenue, as exemption could be obtained by payment of a fee. Certain privileged persons were also exempted. In the time of Edward I, for example, all the men of Lymington were freed of their obligations to mutilate their dogs. Henry III imposed a fine of three shillings on any amusement. Such events drew hugh crowds and special performances were arranged for visiting royalty or heads of State. Special breeds were developed from Mastiff stock for fighting different animals, and the **Bulldog** was designed short enough to rush in under the murderous horns, and with jaws strong enough to clamp and hold.

John Houghton wrote in 1694: 'I have seen a dog tossed by a bull thirty if not forty feet high and the men try to catch them lest the fall might mischief the dog. . . . The true courage and art is for the dog to hold the bull by the nose till he roars, which a courageous bull scorns to do.' The meat from bated bulls was believed to be more tender, because of its exertions prior to death.

Guard Dogs

An earlier account by Barnaby Googe in 1631 shows that Mastiffs were very prized for the guarding of property as well as their fighting skills: 'First the Mastie that keepeth the house; for this purpose you must provide you such a one, as hath a large and mighty body, a great and shrill voyce, that both with his barking he may discover, and with his sight dismay the Theefe, yea, being not seené, with the hooror of his voyce put him to flight. His stature must neither be long nor short, but well set, his lippes blackish, neither turning up, nor hanging too much downe, his mouth blacke and wide, his neatheriawe fat, and coming out of it at either side a fang, appearing more outward than his other teeth; his upper teeth even with his neather not hanging too much over, sharpe and hidden with his lippes, his countenance like a lion,

his brest great and shagayrd, his shoulders broad, his legges bigge, his tail short, his feet very great his disposition must be neither too gentle nor too curst, that he neither fawne upon a theefe, nor lavish of his mouth, barking without cause, neither making it any matter though he be not swift: for he is to fight at home, and to give warning of the enemy.'

From the Mastiff and the Bulldog, the **Bullmastiff** was developed especially as a guard dog. Originally known as the Night Dog because it was the favourite companion of vulnerable nightwatchmen in the mid-19th century, the breed was officially recognized by the Kennel Club in 1924.

The remarks written by Barnaby Googe so many years ago, regarding the temperament and attributes of a guard dog, still hold remarkably true today. The fact that a dog barks and may wake the entire household is generally enough to deter any burglar. With very valuable property, however, larger breeds are specially trained as guards, and the most popular breeds for the job are the **German Shepherd Dog** or **Alsatian**, the **Dobermann** and, more recently, the **Rottweiler**. Potentially, the ideal guard dog is one that is fit, intelligent and has been correctly handled from birth, the same sort of attributes in fact, as needed for police and Army dogs.

Bulldogs being matched in the pit against a captive bear. 1864.

40

A well-bred Dobermann bitch and her
handsome puppy.

Early dogs of war played multiple roles and even drew heavy artillery to the front line.

Left: They also acted as messengers and carried food to troops in the forward trenches.

Modern Dogs of War

In modern warfare, many different breeds of dog have proved their value and, unlike the war dogs of ancient armies, were not expected to fight. The Germans first realized the tremendous potential of war dogs, and from 1870 formulated careful breeding and training programmes, encouraging village dog clubs and organizing matches between them to find the best trained dogs. By the time of the First World War, the German people had over 6000 fully trained war dogs, which between them, saved the lives of more than 4000 German soldiers who would otherwise have died or been made prisoners of war. The British lagged far behind as they had only started dog training in 1910 and, when the United States came into the war, an appeal was sent out for suitable dogs. Instructors were sent from England to America and to France to produce thousands of war dogs. By the outbreak of the Second World War, the Germans had more than 40 000 efficient dogs, and sent half of these to Japan, just prior to their devastating attack on Pearl Harbor in 1941. In 1939 there was a nationwide appeal for dogs and trainers to work with the Royal Air Force and the Army, and the Government Guard Dog School was established. In 1940 the British Army set up a dog school in Belgium and war dogs proved their value time and time again in the following troubled years. **Airedales** and **Boxers** were very good at this type of work, brave and seemingly unaffected by gunfire and shells.

'Judy', a modern war-dog serving with the Royal Air Force, undergoes rigorous training routines.

Above: P.C. Bill Hopkins and 'Blitz', a Rottweiler, in training while Inspector Robert Terry acts as a convincing fugitive from the law.

Far right: At the annual police dog championships dogs and their handlers compete for top awards.

Police Dogs

Dogs are used by the police forces of many countries of the world, and are highly valued for their work. Today, the **German Shepherd Dog** or **Alsatian** is by far the most popular breed for general duties, although the occasional **Rottweiler**, **Dobermann**, or **Weimaraner** might prove ideal for training; **Labradors**, with their exceptional powers of scent discrimination, are favoured for detecting the presence of drugs or explosives.

The first dog used for policing duties was a **Bloodhound** trained to detect sheep stealers in 1805 by the Thrapthon Association for the Prevention of Felons in Northamptonshire. To prove the dog's prowess and to deter would-be sheep stealers, demonstrations of the hound's skills were staged

in which a runner would be given a good start before the dog was put on the line. Even in the worst conditions, the Bloodhound would show itself capable of tracking down the man and as sheep-stealing then carried the death penalty, the crime rate in that area dramatically dropped.

One of the first recorded arrests of a man by a Bloodhound, occurred in the New Forest in 1810. Bloodhounds were used to find bodies as well as to track criminals, and eventually they were trained at a special school near Newbury, Berkshire. As several chief constables kept kennels of the breed, Bloodhounds remained popular policing dogs for several years.

The Alsatian first arrived in Britain during 1911 and a team of such dogs were exhibited at a Kennel Club

Right: Highly trained, this Miami-based police dog guards a fallen rioter during a disturbance.

Police dogs must remain controlled and obedient at all times, even when unleashed and in close proximity to their work-mates.

Show. After the First World War members of the British Forces, highly impressed by the dogs they had observed working as messengers, crossing mine-fields and carrying much-needed Red Cross supplies into dangerous areas, brought some of them home. The dogs were first registered as Alsatian Wolfdogs, because they came from the borders of Germany and Alsace, and were known colloquially as '*Chien Loup*', looking wolf-like, with erect ears.

Breeding and Training Police Dogs

For police work a dog must have certain qualities such as a sound constitution, excellent eyesight, a keen sense of hearing and a strong, discerning sense of smell. It must be highly intelligent with an equable temperament being bold without being aggressive. It is quite important, too, that the dog looks impressive, not in the show sense but in creating an appearance of controlled power. Some police forces

breed their dogs specially, from carefully selected stock, while others rely on gifts of unwanted dogs, usually males about one year old. It has been found that dogs brought up in the normal home environment develop the right sort of temperament for turning into top police dogs. Dogs donated to the police are given a rigorous veterinary screening which includes an X-ray test to detect the possible presence of Hip Dysplasia, a congenital defect in the sockets of the hip girdle to which

Alsatians are particularly prone.

The student police dog is about 12–18 months old and physically mature when it commences its training programme. Great attention is paid to suiting each dog to its handler, to ensure that a long-term compatible relationship will be possible, for the pair are likely to be together for eight years or more. The young dog moves into the handler's home at the beginning of training and soon becomes integrated into the family.

The dog and his handler build up to a supreme degree of coordination, trust and affection.

47

The first steps in training concentrate on obedience work. The dog learns heelwork, first on the lead and then with the lead removed. It learns to sit, stand and go down on command, and both voice and hand signals are taught. When the dog is proficient at these exercises on and off the lead, it learns to stay when told to do so, and to answer the recall command, trotting back to sit in front of the handler. Before long the dog works well at a distance, responding to all the handler's commands promptly and with an obvious desire to please. The dog is taught to retrieve, and is given jumping lessons to help develop its natural agility. It must be able to scale a high board, hurdles and jump both long and low.

All these exercises are taught in a slow methodical and progressive manner, ensuring that the dog is never asked to do more than it can at any stage. In this way the police dog is gradually built up in fitness, ability and mental comprehension, and in working so closely each day with its own handler, the unique human-dog bond is formed. Two of the most difficult exercises that the dog must learn are the 'send-away' and 'redirection'. The send-away must be mastered first and the dog is taught to go off at a good speed in a straight line following the direction indicated, and it must not stop until told to do so. Once the dog is going away and being recalled without making any mistakes, the redirection exercises are taught, and the animal learns to go left or right on command, while working at a distance from the handler.

Advanced basic training for the police dog includes tracking. Every dog has an acute sense of smell and in the police dog, this is developed so that it can follow the trail of a human. The dog does not follow one particular scent, but a complex combination which its brain assesses and evaluates. A track scent may be any combination of a number of factors such as a very subtle personal odour, which is as unique to every human as his fingerprints. His clothes too will give off distinctive odours whether they are of wool, cotton or synthetics, and there are occupational scents such as food, oil, or cement dust, and footwear odours of leather, rubber, plastics and shoe polish. Other scent factors arise from crushed vegetation and crushed soil animals such as tiny insects, both caused by normal footfalls, and the

Left and below: Even experienced police dogs keep in shape with regular training sessions.

48

softer the ground, the stronger the scent perceived by the tracker dog.

For tracking, the dog wears a special harness of leather or webbing attached to a very long tracking line so that it can work well in advance of its trainer and it is taught slowly and methodically to follow all manner of trails, fresh laid at first, progressing gradually to older tracks over difficult terrain. While working on a trail a dog may come across an article of clothing or stolen property, thrown away by the fugitive, so the trainee dog is taught to halt or drop into the down

Top left: 'Shadow' waits at heel for the next command from his handler, P.C. Tom Bowles.

Top right: 'Blitz' shows his prowess and agility in clearing the high boards.

Above: This Rottweiler is an excellent tracker dog and waits expectantly as his special harness is fitted.

position if it discovers any such thing during its exercises. Police dogs also learn to comb areas in systematic search patterns to find articles. Small items are picked up and taken to the handler, larger, irretrievable items are indicated by an excited bark. The dogs learn to seek out hidden humans, too, and when they have located the person, they must not attack, but stay close and indicate their whereabouts by barking.

The police dog is taught to attack only on command, and when given the instruction will chase the suspect and grasp his fore-arm firmly, holding on until told to leave by the handler. In training, an assistant wearing a leather arm shield acts the part of the suspect, and the dog is encouraged to bite hard and cleanly at the fore-arm, never at any other part of the body. A good dog rarely shows aggression at this time, it attacks and bites only when ordered and immediately releases its grip when told to do so. The dog is also taught to chase a running suspect, but to stand off, circle and bark at him when he stops and stands still. This is very difficult to teach to the keen dog who would much rather bite the man's arm. As the dog progresses, it is taught how to attack under gunfire, and how to disarm someone trying to beat him off with a stout stick. Some police dogs, generally Labradors or other retrievers, prove particularly suitable for

seeking out drugs or explosives. Dogs trained in this sphere are taught to concentrate on particular substances, and specialist dogs may be called on by police forces of other areas to carry out their unique duties.

Police dogs must be trained carefully in crowd control work, and on command will bark at or circle around groups of humans. Many people think that such dogs are vicious and dangerous, but nothing could be farther from the truth. Handlers, accompanied by their dogs, pay instructional visits to schools, where the children are encouraged to make friends with the animals, and all police dogs are screened for their steady temperament and reliability in all circumstances. Although fully trained, the police dog and handler continue their regular training exercises and routines so that they always remain at peak fitness, ready to deal with any situation that might occur.

Security and Prison Dogs

Dogs for security work start their training in much the same way as the police dog, but are expected to respond to several handlers, rather than just one. Dogs are carefully screened for fitness and those with any sign of nervousness in their temperament are discarded. They are taught to climb high walls, to pass through restricted spaces and to jump through fire.

Above: The tracker dog is given the scent in a search for an escaped prisoner.

Prison dogs are really guard dogs in reverse for they exist to prevent escape from rather than entry into the premises. Originally prison dogs were selected for their propensity to bite, but in the 1960s, a national scheme for training came into force. The trial scheme was conducted at London's Brixton prison, and seven dogs took part, first being trained by police methods then transferred to modern kennels within the prison confines. Within a short while it became apparent that the constraints of prison life were affecting the physical and mental health of the dogs, and a new system was introduced whereby each dog was worked by one handler with whom he lived when off duty. As in the police force, the prison dog and his handler become a united, inseparable team throughout the working life of the dog, and on its retirement, the dog may remain as a family pet, while a younger canine recruit takes over his work, or he may go to another approved home for the remainder of his life.

Although the German Shepherd is by far the most popular breed for police and security work, the Rottweiler has been found to show all the desired characteristics, although its special temperament needs a carefully selected, understanding handler. It is a very powerful dog indeed and has a wide, mastiff-like jaw armed with formidable teeth.

The Rottweiler is a very old breed, descended from Mastiff-type dogs used in the Middle Ages for hunting wild boar. As such hunting declined, the breed came into its own as a drover's dog and still performs this function in some countries. The breed was originally called the Rottweiler Metzgerhund – the Butchers' Dog of Rottweil, and the cattle drovers would tie their money pouches to the dogs' collars to prevent them being taken by thieves. Imported to both Britain and the United States in the 1930s, the sturdy black-and-tan dogs are strong and sound, making valued family pets and guards as well as working dogs.

Draught Dogs

Opposite page, top: Extremely hardy and wearing a natural weather-proof coat, the husky withstands sub-zero temperatures and biting winds.

Opposite page, below: A dog team rests in the shadow of the Rocky Mountains in Alberta, Canada.

Below: Huskies have proved invaluable as sled-dogs on numerous expeditions in both the Arctic and Antarctic.

There are two main categories of dogs used for draught work, the Spitz varieties found in cold countries and stockier dogs, often of Mastiff descent, which are used in warmer countries. Of the two types, the Spitz group is better known, and of the many breeds used for sled work, the most famous are the **Eskimo Dog** or **Huskie**, the **Alaskan Malamute** and the **Siberian Husky**. Such dogs have been used for generations, for without them human settlements in many remote regions would have been impossible.

Sled-dogs

In the 14th century, Ibn Batuta wrote this account of travel in Mongolia: 'In that country they travel only with small vehicles drawn by great dogs. For the steppe is covered with ice, and the feet of men or the shoes of horses would slip, whereas the dogs having claws their paws don't slip upon the ice. . . . The guide of the travellers is a dog who has often made the journey before. The price of such a beast is sometimes as high as a thousand donars or thereabouts. He is yoked to the vehicle by the neck, and three other dogs are harnessed along with him. He is the chief, and all the other dogs with their carts follow his guidance and stop when he stops. The master of this animal never ill-uses him or scolds him and at feeding time the dogs are always served before the men. If this be not attended to, the chief of the dogs will get sulky and run off, leaving the master to perdition.'

The best sled-dogs are short and stocky with powerful chest muscles enabling them to pull a weight of around 300 lb (660 kg) over a distance of 35 miles (56 km) or so. The Siberian Husky is considered the superior breed for both pulling power and stamina, and like all sled-dogs seems to thrive and work on a diet that would be disdained by most pet dogs. Although they have a reputation for extreme aggressiveness, Huskies of all sorts respond well to their training and work with a will. They have a strict pack order within the team, which the handler must understand, respect and use in order to get the best out of his dogs.

The Eskimos have a purely working relationship with their dogs. They understand them well but have no feeling of sentimentality towards them. In winter the animals are well fed and worked hard, but in summer, when food may be scarce, the dogs are half starved.

Dog teams, consisting mainly of Malamutes or Greenland Huskies, are trained carefully and great pride is taken in fitting them with comfortable and efficient harness, designed to get

the maximum pulling power from the least effort. The sleds are streamlined and the runners kept in good condition so that they move easily over the snow and ice with minimum drag. When the dogs are between four and five years of age they are killed for meat and their hides used for lining sealskin boots, mittens and hoods. As each member of a team reaches its retirement age it is replaced by a younger dog, and the relative positions of dogs within the team are changed until the best working combination is achieved. As the 14th century report showed, the presence of a 'king' dog is of utmost importance in the team, keeping fighting to the minimum and ordering the social structure of the group which is, in essence, a small pack.

In northern Canada sled teams are used to deliver mail and urgent supplies to remote regions and are still the favoured form of transport for fur-trappers and traders. The Royal Canadian Mounted Police has always used teams of well-bred, carefully fed and meticulously trained Huskies to help them in covering the Northwest Territories.

Right: A team of Siberian Huskies competing in a sled-dog race.

Below: Huskies beach a boat on the Snake River, Nome, Alaska.

The nomadic Chuchi tribes of northeastern Siberia use sled-dogs for pulling and as efficient hunters and fearless guards. These people have always enjoyed close relationships with their dogs, which are recognized by the American Kennel Club as Siberian Huskies. The breed has been kept pure, and although smaller than other Husky breeds is valued for important expedition work and general haulage in icy regions.

At the turn of this century, in the era of the Great Gold Rush, the miners spent their off-duty hours drinking and racing their dog teams against each other. The Nome Kennel Club was formed in 1907 and a course covering over 400 miles (640 km) across country was devised, with a grand prize of $10 000 offered to the winner. Goosak, a Russian Trader, imported a team of Siberian Huskies for the 1908 race and had to suffer a variety of taunts and jeers from fellow competitors comparing the small stature of his team against their larger, fiercer Malamutes. The bookmakers offered odds of 100 to 1 against the Chuchi dogs even finishing the gruelling run. However, Goosak came in a close third overall, despite the fact that he was totally snow blind for the last few miles. In following years teams of Sib-

erian Huskies have run the great race with performances which belie their smaller size, always putting up superb performances and often winning.

In 1925 Nome was hit by a severe epidemic of diphtheria, and dog teams were employed to run relays carrying the life-saving serum from Anchorage, a total distance of 658 miles (1059 km). The conditions were appalling, including an 80 mph (129 km/h) blizzard. It was to take five days for the serum to get through. As the days and hours ticked by, Nome's great dog-team driver, Leonard Seppala, set out to meet the incoming team. His team of Siberian Huskies had to travel over 80 miles (129 km) in one day, with the temperature at 30°F below zero (−34°C). On the following day he had almost given up hope when he intercepted the incoming relay team at the point of exhaustion. Seppala and his lead dog called 'Togo' have since become legendary figures in Husky history books.

As the technological age devised special forms of mechanized transport to replace dog teams in icy regions, it was feared that the sled-dogs breeds would decline. However, a form of racing has become so popular in Canada and the northern United States that their future is assured. Sled racing is an ideal winter sport for the whole family and clubs exist which hold weekend meets for training sessions and racing. Children are encouraged to start with small teams of three or four dogs while adults handle teams of ten or 12. With experience, the team handlers can acquire the skills necessary to enter the big events where competition is fierce and a carefully selected and well-trained team is essential. During their early training in the summer months, sled-dogs pull small carts fitted with wheels instead of runners. They become accustomed to the soft leather or nylon harness and learn to use their shoulders for maximum pulling power. They are taught to respond to their handler's voice and learn many words of instruction and encouragement. The basic words of command include 'Haw' to turn to the left and 'Gee' to turn to the right. As the team begins to work well together, each dog's fitness is built up by careful feeding and regular working sessions through each week until they are ready for the start of the racing season.

Above: A St. Bernard playing as sled-dog on the ski slopes.

Above right: Here two massive St. Bernards draw a flower wagon at a Swiss festival.

Right: This interesting engraving shows a variety of dogs being used for draught work by a vegetable vendor in Antwerp, Belgium during the last century.

Draught Dogs

In 1820 John Lawrence reported that a Monsieur Chabert had arrived in London from Bath in the company of a great Siberian wolf-dog which, it was claimed, could draw that gentleman's gig more than 30 miles (48 km) a day. This was an unusual form of canine haulage, but dogs have been used for general draught work for centuries in many parts of the world. Small traders of Switzerland and the Low Countries used dogs to draw light carts loaded with their wares, and generally chose animals of Mastiff type, strong but gentle and with the sort of temperament that was steady, but did not encourage friendly advances from strangers.

It is obvious that dogs were used extensively for such purposes in other parts of Western Europe, too, for in 1576 Abraham Fleming wrote about a useful dog described by him as a 'tinckers curre'. Having observed its use he said 'With marveilous pacience they beare bigge budgettes fraught with tinckers tooles, and metall meete to mend kettles, porridge pots, skellets and chafers, and other such like trumpery requisite for their occupacion and loytering trade, easing him of a great burden which otherwise he himself should carry upon his shoulders. . . .'

Dog-drawn carts carried fish from the seaports to the railway stations and markets in Britain. Some dogs were harnessed as teams of four and one such team of **Newfoundlands** is said to have been capable of drawing a load from Brighton to Portsmouth in one day. By 1839 draught dogs were banned in central London because they were considered by the Metropolitan Police to cause unnecessary traffic problems, and eventually the use of dogs as draught animals was stopped altogether throughout the country.

Draught dogs continued their valuable work in other countries, however, and were used to deliver every type of merchandise from bread, milk, fruit and other foodstuffs, to coal and wood for fuel. The European draught dogs were always valued and well-cared for by their owners and subjected to regular inspections by local authority officials. Loads were always carefully regulated, and the harness checked for condition, kindness and suitability. It was ruled that dogs had to be of a size suitable to carry out their work, and pregnant or nursing bitches were banned from employment. It was ordered that dogs were provided with waterproof coats and warm blankets for adverse weather conditions, and given proper rest periods. Although it is very rare to see working draught dogs these days except in very isolated and remote villages, the dogs themselves seem to love their jobs and always look very fit and contented.

Rescue Dogs

In recent years there has been an increase in the number of dogs being trained for mountain rescue work, and most countries with high or remote mountain regions have their own efficiently trained rescue teams, equipped and ready for any emergency. Although **Collies**, **Labradors** and some crossbreds have proved very able at the work, the **German Shepherd Dog** predominates. The Rescue or Avalanche Dogs of today generally belong to volunteer civilians, and both dog and owner must pass fitness and aptitude tests before being accepted for training. Owner and dog must be fit and strong enough to cope with all types of adverse weather conditions and terrain, and the dog must be psychologically sound and responsive to all forms of training. It must be completely safe with all other animals and not likely to be distracted by any game encountered during its work.

When they are accepted for training, the owner and his dog receive instruction and exercises similar to those given to police dogs and their handlers. An intensive course in 'nose work' follows until the dog is able to locate a person buried under as much as 10 ft (3 metres) of snow. Dogs must be able to work in darkness as well as in daylight, and undergo a probationary period followed by an advanced aptitude test before qualifying as a full member of the rescue team. All members of the team train and practice regularly and the dogs also undergo periodical tests to ensure that their efficiency is maintained at a very high level.

Dogs have proved their worth in rescue operations on many occasions. They are able to locate buried persons very quickly indeed, then dig them out, at the same time barking furiously to bring human aid. This speed in location is vital and may mean the difference between life or death for the victim of an avalanche or blizzard. Dogs are invaluable in tracking and finding lost climbers, too, and in the Welsh Mountains, the Search and Dog Rescue Association has introduced its

dogs to special harnesses which allow them to be airlifted by helicopter whenever necessary.

Historically the most famous of all rescue dogs is the massive **St. Bernard**, the ancestors of which are said to have been the huge Mollossus dogs brought by Romans armies as guards, when they pushed their frontiers north as far as Lake Geneva, building highways and passes for the safe transport of their legions in their battles against the Huns.

One of the passes made by the Romans some 2000 years ago was in the valley of Aosta, and was known as the *Summum Penninus*. It formed an important way through the mountains linking Italy and the countries of the North. Even in the days of the Romans the pass was of great significance and was the site of a great temple raised to the glory of Jupiter. Eventually a young nobleman named Bernard de Menthon came to the pass and, in 962, erected an Augustinian monastery. First named in honour of St. Nicholas, it was renamed after its founder's death as the Hospice of the Great Saint Bernard. In the chapel at the Hospice is a picture of the founder

Saint with his dog, but it was not until 1665 that dogs were first trained by the monks for use in mountain rescue work. Dogs for the monastery were chosen with care from villages in the Pennine Alps and the Bernese Oberland. All from good mountaineering stock, they were selected for strength, hardiness and obedience, and for the special sort of short but dense coat, suitable for working in snow. At first the dogs were a motley bunch, but gradually a definite type emerged: first called the Alpine Dog, then Alpine Mastiff, then the Hospice Dog. Eventually, *circa* 1880, its name was finally changed to the St. Bernard. It has been estimated that in the past 300 years or so, the dogs from the Hospice have been directly responsible for saving the lives of more than 2000 people. The most famous dog, 'Barry', was credited with having saved 40 travellers, and in making his 41st rescue attempt was killed by the traveller who mistook the big dog for a wolf.

The monks used their trained dogs to help in searching for lost travellers, after avalanches and snow storms, and it was a general routine in any weather to send out a pair of dogs to patrol a route 14 km to the north towards Martigny, and another pair to track in the opposite direction towards the Italian town of Aosta. The dogs were trained to go to a rest hut, then to turn and retrace their steps to the Hospice. If they met anyone on the way, they would attempt to induce them back to the Hospice. Only dogs were kept at the Hospice, the bitches and puppies being housed at the monastery at Martigny, and the dogs always warned the monks of the coming of a blizzard at least half an hour before it struck.

Today, few people use the upper pass, as a road tunnel has been cut through the mountains, and only two or three dogs stay at the Hospice in the winter months, being kept in confined runs, their rescue function now obsolete. The Hospice is now run as a hotel, and the monastic section houses a museum of Roman artifacts and a library. The monks have modern rescue vehicles, and are expert skiers. However, in other very remote regions of the world, like Tibet, descendants of the famous Swiss dogs still carry out mountain rescue duties.

Above: Monks of the Hospice of the Great St. Bernard with their famous rescue dogs.

Opposite page: Young St. Bernard dogs undergoing preliminary training in mountain rescue techniques, finding 'bodies' under heavy snow.

Guide Dogs

Guide Dogs

Although dogs have been used over many years for guiding and leading blind masters, old prints and drawings show that this was in a rather aimless and haphazard way, the dog's motivation being devotion, hunger or the need for a sheltered place in which to rest. It is only in comparatively recent times that dogs have been *trained* to act as guides.

Guide Dog Training Centres

In 1819 a book was published setting out the basic principles of scientific training for dogs to lead the blind. It was written by Herr Johann Lein, the Founder of the Institute for the Blind in Vienna, but was obviously too ad-

vanced for its day, for nothing further was done in this field of study for almost another century. The first serious and methodical training of dogs as guides began as the result of an incident in Germany in 1916. A doctor was walking in the hospital grounds with a wounded and blinded soldier, when he was called away. He left his **Alsatian** guard dog with the patient, and when it started to rain heavily, the dog led the sightless man back to the shelter of the buildings. The doctor was so impressed by this natural, protective behaviour in the dog, that he decided to start a special school in order to train other dogs to guide the vast numbers of casualties blinded during the First World War. By 1925

A blind water-carrier of the last century is guided by his faithful dog.

the school had been adopted by the German Red Cross, and news of the success of the venture began to spread around the world.

Meanwhile, during the 1920s, an American woman, Mrs. Harrison Eustis founded a training establishment at Mount Pelerin in Switzerland. Named the Fortunate Fields Kennels, it aimed at breeding and training Alsatian dogs for the use of Swiss and Italian Police forces, for customs duties, and work with the army. Mrs. Eustis heard of the German work in training dogs as guides for the blind and having visited the centre at Potsdam, wrote an enthusiastic article for the American Magazine, *The Saturday Evening Post*.

Mrs. Eustis received many letters in response to her article, including one from Morris Frank, a young blind American, imploring her to help him find a suitable guide dog. He planned to return to America, once he had obtained this dog, and to try to arouse interest in the work, with the aim of providing guide dogs for other blind people. Mrs. Eustis arranged for Mr. Humphrey, one of her trainers, to go

Young trainee guide dogs are given lots of play periods and encouraged to socialize.

to the centre at Potsdam in order to study their methods, and when he returned a centre was set up for the training of instructors and for teaching both guide dogs and blind people to work confidently together. The School was called *L'Oeil qui Voit* or The Seeing Eye. Mr. Humphrey personally selected and trained 'Buddy' for Morris Frank, who in 1928 became the first American to own a guide dog. He wrote a book in praise of his beloved bitch and called it 'The First Lady of the Seeing Eye'. Mrs. Eustis was tireless in her work, travelling extensively, lecturing and writing articles, all inspired by her belief in the worthwhile future of dogs for leading the blind. In 1930 her articles appeared in English journals, and one prompted a letter to the *Liverpool Echo* imploring someone to help train a guide dog for a blind man in Liverpool. Miss Muriel Crooke avidly read the articles and correspondence; she was a breeder of Alsatians and a successful competitor with them in obedience tests and trials. Before long she was on her way to visit Mr. Musgrave Frankland, secretary of the National Institute for the Blind in Liverpool.

Eventually Miss Crooke and a small group of interested friends met Mrs. Eustis in London on 23 September 1930, and discussed plans for the establishment of training centres in Britain. Although Mrs. Eustis had met some opposition during her visit to St. Dunstan's, the blind persons' rehabilitation centre, the National Institute for the Blind expressed keen interest in the scheme, so she decided to loan one of her best trainers to the British group so that a trial unit could be started without further delay.

The Guide Dog Committee was formed and became affiliated to the National Institute for the Blind, fund-raising activities began and a piece of land in Wallasey was loaned as a training ground. A humble lock-up garage was rented for use as dog-room and store and everything was ready. Mr. Debetaz, the trainer from *L'Oeil qui Voit*, arrived in England in July 1931, accompanied by Mr. Humphrey who was to select suitable dogs for training. The first group of 28 Alsatian bitches arrived in Wallasey, and after being given stringent aptitude tests, seven were chosen as suitable candidates. All but one of these seven bitches were given as gifts to the movement, and all expenses were kept to the very minimum for the first course.

Mrs. Eustis donated her trainer's wages, so the only outlay was for his board and lodgings, and the food, equipment and kennelling of the dogs. After the first stages of training were completed, Mr. Humphrey returned to Britain in order to test the dogs, and they all came through with flying colours. Of the five blind men who applied for dogs, four proved satisfactory and after completing their lengthy training period, left with their own 'seeing eyes'. Six months later, their probationary period was over and all four men furnished glowing reports on the progress of themselves and their dogs. Four more men and their guide dogs were successfully trained in 1932 and, with the support of Lady Schuster who dedicated the rest of her life to the movement, fund-raising efforts were increased to enable future plans to be laid. In October 1933 Captain Nikolai Liakhoff arrived in Britain. A former officer of the Russian Imperial Guard, he was a skilled dog trainer and took control of the classes. The following year, when the Guide Dog Committee joined forces with the Tail-waggers' Club, the British Guide Dogs for the Blind Association was formed and Captain Liakhoff was appointed its first training Director. The Tail-waggers' offices in London were taken over for use by the Association, and for the continuance of training, a house near the seashore in Wallasey was rented for a nominal sum. Staff and students were housed here, and some kennels were built in the grounds. Work was hampered by the outbreak of war, and the Association's house was destroyed by bombs, but eventually Edmondscote Manor in Leamington Spa was purchased, converted and set up as the movement's first permanent training centre. A second centre was opened in Exeter in 1950 and in 1961, the first purpose-built and meticulously designed training centre was finished in Bolton. Since then the fourth centre emerged in Forfar, Scotland in 1965, and a fifth, at Wokingham, Berkshire in 1977. The five centres are all run on similar lines, with qualified instructors to teach blind people to live with and be led by their guide dogs.

Opposite page: Blind deaconess Helen Starns with her guide dog 'Prisca'.

The trained guide dog instils its owner with complete confidence, even when crossing busy roads.

Training Guide Dogs and Their Masters

Although the Association will consider any registered blind person over 17 years of age for training, applicants are required to meet certain standards. They must be capable of walking properly, must be able to hear clearly and be able to show that their home environment is suitable for keeping a dog. Blind people accepted for training must attend a residential course at one of the Association's centres. The course lasts at least four weeks, during which time a blind person learns to handle the dog, to care for it in all ways including feeding and grooming, and to understand the animal's needs. Each student is taught the commands and control of his dog, and learns to read all the signals the dog gives in every situation. The working relationship between the student and the dog is encouraged and helped by an experienced trainer.

For the first two days of the course, the trainer takes the part of the dog so that the student can get the feel of handling the harness. Great care is taken in pairing up dogs and students, and the animals are chosen for their potential in suiting each individual student's requirements. Having retired to their individual rooms, the students wait with a mixture of anticipation and anxiety for their dogs to be brought to them for the first time.

Above: Learning to wear the special guiding handle is an important part of the training programme.

Right: In early lessons on busy pavements, the dog is worked in tandem, with two trainers teaching vitally important points.

The meeting can be very emotional, for many blind students have waited for many months for just this moment. Having introduced the dog to its new owner, the trainer leaves the pair to get acquainted. From this moment, the blind person is expected to assume all responsibility for his dog's feeding, grooming and exercising. and the animal will sleep in the student's room at night. During the next few weeks, the dog's affection is gradually transferred from the trainer to the student, who begins to gain confidence in the correct and efficient handling of his new guide. The trainer takes great care to ensure that the dog does not suffer from accidental mishandling, and that its training and confidence is not damaged or impaired in any way. Eventually the student is pronounced ready to go home along with his new friend and companion, and is given extra confidence by having regular visits from an instructor, to help in all ways, including the formation of suitable routes around the neighbourhood. The guide dog has a full health check before leaving the centre, and this is followed up by regular six-monthly checks from a veterinary surgeon local to its new home. All newly trained guide-dog owners are required to submit a monthly progress report to the Association.

Although it costs a lot of money to breed, rear and train a fully fledged guide dog, and to teach the blind person to care for and handle it correctly, the ownership of the dog passes to the blind person for a very nominal fee. The money for the training comes from voluntary contributions, and fund-raising appeals are made throughout the year.

The British Guide Dogs for the Blind Association now has its own breeding and puppy walking centre, so that it can produce a regular supply of puppies from carefully selected parents. Almost 100 bitches and several stud dogs are kept, all chosen for physical and temperamental soundness. About 85 per cent of today's guide dogs are **Labrador Retrievers**, both yellow and black, but some other breeds are favoured, including the **Alsatian** or **German Shepherd Dog**, the **Golden Retriever**, the **Boxer** and the **Border Collie**, and very occasionally certain crosses between these breeds are accepted if they are physically and mentally suited to the work expected of them. Most of the animals chosen for training are bitches, as they

are generally less aggressive than male dogs and also less likely to be distracted from the important job at hand. All guide dogs are neutered by spaying or castration before their training commences. When a suitable puppy reaches six to eight weeks of age, it is checked for fitness, then goes to live with a puppy-walker living near to the centre. A puppy walker is a special sort of person who has a naturally confident and sensible attitude to dogs. She is generally the mother in an ordinary family, and is prepared to give basic training to a young dog for a period of about nine months. During this time the puppy must learn house manners, to be clean and tidy indoors and to be generally obedient. It must be taught to walk on the left-hand side, and slightly in front of the handler, and must be acclimatized to busy streets, traffic and crowds. The puppy must be kept in good health and only allowed to learn the lessons required

Here a dog is preventing its newly acquired blind mistress from stepping into the path of a moving vehicle, while a trainer stands by.

by the training centre. Then, when it has reached ten to 12 months of age, its future potential as a guide dog is assessed, and it is taken back by the Association for its formal training. The puppy-walker is always upset when her dog is taken away, but is usually compensated in some measure by having the opportunity to take on another youngster in its place.

When the young dog has completed its period of home-life training, it is tested both physically and mentally. It is important that it has attained a height of at least 19 inches (48 cm) at the shoulder, so that the necessary balance between dog and owner may be maintained. The dog must be intelligent and obviously eager to please, physically sound and totally free from any nervousness, aggression or viciousness. It must be responsive, but not so sensitive that it jumps at the slightest touch. In the early days, the rejection rate was very high at this stage of the selection process, now, thanks to the careful breeding policy of the Association, this rate has dramatically dropped. Once a dog has

passed the stringent selection tests, it has its basic training polished up, learning to respond accurately and promptly to the simple commands of 'sit', 'down' and 'come'. It must walk in the centre of the pavement and sit down at the kerb without being told. It is accustomed to its harness, and when its confidence is apparent, it is then handed over to a qualified trainer.

Now the young dog has to learn spatial awareness, it must judge both height and width, and be able to cope with traffic near at hand and approaching from a distance. These lessons are difficult to teach and the six-month training period is very necessary to ensure that every lesson has been thoroughly absorbed. If any dog seems unhappy with its training and appears unwilling to want to please its trainer, it is immediately discarded from the training programme. The dogs are not worked in harness for long periods, and are given as much free-running time as possible to keep them fresh, alert and fit. The dog is taught that the fitting of the harness

The trainee guide dog must learn to avoid all types of obstacles.

Lessons are first taught on the lead by a sighted trainer.

means work-time, and that it must carry out its routines to the letter, but when the harness is taken off, it is free-time and it may behave just like any other family pet.

The guide dog is different from any other trained dog in that it is able to bring itself to override a command when it knows better than its owner. If it is told to go forward, for example, and it can see the approach of a fast-moving vehicle, it will disobey the command and wait for the road to clear before moving forward.

It takes about a year for a blind person and his dog to merge into a perfect partnership and, in this time, the owner becomes skilled in the care of the dog, while the dog learns regular routes and its owner's habits. The working life of a guide dog is about nine or ten years, and on retirement, the dog may be kept by the owner, or allowed to live out the rest of its life with a close friend or relative. Some partnerships form very close bonds indeed, and as their dogs grow older

such owners worry constantly about the impending parting, for even the promise of a new guide dog cannot compensate for the threat of losing an old friend.

Those blind people who are lucky enough to have guide dogs, benefit psychologically as well as being able to enjoy increased mobility. The dog encourages sighted people to stop and chat, providing as it does a suitable conversation opener. The guide-dog owner is compelled to exercise the dog and in so doing, takes more health-giving exercise himself. He can go out whenever he wants to do so, secure in the knowledge that his dog will guide him and return him safely home again. The Guide Dog pamphlet says 'For those people who for years have had to rely on sighted escorts to take them out, ownership of a guide dog brings freedom and independence. The harness handle, the vital connection between the blind person and the dog, is the link that leads to a new way of life.'

Coursing and Racing Dogs

The running dogs or gaze-hounds have a longer history than those which hunt by scent alone, and the familiar Greyhound of today, along with the Afghan Hound, Borzoi, Saluki and Whippet are directly descended from the old Arabian Greyhound.

Greyhounds

The Greyhound was a popular dog in the days of Ancient Egypt and on a stela found near the tomb of the Great Antef at Thebes, dated about 3000 B.C., there is a representation of the King standing with his four favourite Greyhounds beside him. The hieroglyphs give the names of the dogs as the Gazelle, the Greyhound, the Black, and the Firepot. The Abbott Papyrus, written in the time of Rameses IX and now housed in the British Museum, mentions the tomb of Antef, describing him as a worthy king who is shown on a tablet, standing with a dog named 'Behukaa' between his feet. The Slughi or Great Greyhound of the Egyptian Pharaohs was exceedingly swift and graceful, and its lineal descendants have been used for succeeding centuries to hunt the desert gazelle.

Of the 22 types of hounds described by the Roman scholar Gratius Faliscus in his *Cyngeticon Liber*, one is the Veltragus, which is most likely to be the Greyhound.

'Would you chase the deer
Or urge the motions of the
   smaller hare,
Let the brisk greyhounds of the
   Celtic name
Bound o'er the glebe and show
   his pointed frame,
Swift as the wish that darts the
   wind along.'

It is thought that the 'sight' hounds travelled with the Celtic tribes in their progress from the east to the west, eventually reaching Britain in two streams, one from neighbouring Gaul, and the other from further eastwards, reaching the British Isles by crossing the North Sea. The Roman legions in Britain had their own Greyhounds, many descended from Arabian stock, and these would undoubtedly have bred with dogs from villages near the garrisons.

The Romans valued their British-bred hounds of Germanic and Celtic bloodlines. Olympius Nemesianus wrote: 'Britain, divided from the Continent by seas, sent the fleetest hounds, the best the wide world over, for the chase.' And an epitaph still survives which underlines the Romans' love for their prized and faithful hounds:

'Gaul was my birthplace and I was called after a rich seashell being given a name which became my beauty. Fearlessly I would draw the perilous coverts and hunt through the mountain ways the savage quarry. I was white and never knew heavy chains or blows of the cruel whip, for I lay soft on my master's breast and when I tired I laid me down upon his bed. I ran silent and none there were who feared my brawling tongue.'

Opposite page, top: Alert, long-legged hounds from a relief on the ancient Egyptian temple at Kom Ombo.

Opposite page, bottom: Early French hounds, possibly the ancestors of the Talbots. British Museum, London.

Below: Prince Abdullah Khan Uzbeck (A.D. 991–1006) rides out with his falcon-master and accompanying greyhound. Victoria and Albert Museum, London.

By the beginning of the 6th century, external invasions of Britain had ceased, and during the reign of King Canute, a set of forest laws were passed. These imposed heavy fines on any individual found keeping Greyhounds, unless he was possessed of land yielding £100 per annum, or that the animals were so mutilated that they were unable to hunt. The disabling operation referred to entailed the cutting of the tendons at the back of the dog's legs.

Charlemagne, Emperor of the Holy Roman Empire, passed strict laws relating to dogs, legislating particularly against the keeping of such animals in monasteries, but was fond of having quality hounds of his own and was often presented with such animals as gifts. In the epic poem, *The Song of Roland*, the Saracen Ambassador says,

'Thus speaks the King, Marsilion great in rule,
Much hath he studied the saving faith and true.
Now of his wealth he would send you in sooth
Lions and bears, leashed greyhounds not a few.'

Hywel Dda of Wales in his detailed law codes of 948 refers to the Greyhound in the determination of bloodprices for 'sight' hounds.

It seems that abbots and abbesses were so passionately fond of hunting, coursing and other sports, that they often allowed their ecclesiastical duties to lapse, and through the centuries various laws were passed to curb these pursuits, though often to no avail.

Coursing with hounds was always a very popular pastime and Edward III delighted in the sport. He enjoyed an annual challenge match between his own dogs and those of William Clown, Abbot of Leicester, then considered a foremost authority on coursing and related sports. Clown, excusing himself to his critics, wrote,

'I would not have taken delight in the frivolity of such hunting if it had not been solely for displaying civility to the Lords of the Kingdom, to gain their goodwill and to obtain favour in the business affairs of the abbey.'

In those days, coursing consisted of taking out hounds and hunting for hare, setting one dog against another, with wagers being placed on the skill and speed of the favourite. Such dogs were highly prized by royalty and the clergy.

The great British poet, Geoffrey Chaucer, is thought to have been still

Above: Early bloodhounds join their greyhound companions at the kill. Musée Condé, Chantilly.

Above right: A white greyhound solicits scraps from his master's servant. Biblioteca Marciana, Venice.

Right: A pack of greyhounds bravely tackle a ferocious wild boar.

working on his unfinished *Canterbury Tales* at the time of his death in 1400. He wrote of many dogs, and in the Monk's Tale says:

'The rule of Good St. Benet of St. Maur
as old and strict he tended to ignore
This monk was therefore as a good man to house
Greyhounds he had, as swift as birds, to course.'

The Cluniac Code, passed in 1485, was designed to prevent those of holy orders from keeping hounds and other dogs, ordering 'neither dogs nor puppies which defile the monastries and oftentimes trouble the service of God by their barking and sometimes tear the Church Books.'

During the 15th century the selective breeding of dogs was practised with great skill and care, and Edward, Duke of York, who was later killed at the Battle of Agincourt in 1415, wrote and published England's first manual on hunting and related sports, called *The Master of Game*. The text describes all breeds of hounds at that time and gives advice on their breeding, general care and training. English dogs were coveted by sportsmen the world over and were often given as diplomatic gifts to dignitaries overseas.

In 1471 the Duke of Milan sent his ambassador to England bearing the following letter, 'We desire you to obtain some fine English hackneys of those called 'hobby' for the use of ourself and the Duchess our consort, as well as some Greyhounds for our hunting, a laudable exercise in which we take great delight, and so we have decided to send you to England where we understand that each of these things is very plentiful and of rare excellence. We are giving you a thousand gold ducats for the purpose to buy the best and finest horses you can find and dogs also. In order that you may find and buy them more easily we are sending with you El Rossetto, our master of the horse, and two of our dog-keepers who know our tastes and the quality of the horses and dogs that we require.'

The opening of the East India Company increased trade between Britain and the Orient, and many fine British dogs were exported. In 1614 a letter to the Company asked them to procure 'a fine Greyhound' for the son of a Japanese customer, and it is probable that English Greyhounds reached China, too, at about the same time.

Greyhound Coursing

The sport of coursing is even older than that of fox hunting, and the first rules for the conduct of public meetings were codified during the reign of Queen Elizabeth I. In Turbeville's *Booke of Hunting* he mentions the coursing of hares with hounds dating back to 1576, but such events were private sporting occasions between friends. The first public coursing meeting occurred in 1776, and was a well-attended affair held at the invitation of Lord Orford at the market town of Swaffham in the County of Norfolk.

The method of judging these early meetings was described: ' . . . and for the better deciding of all these questions, if it be a solemn assembly, they use to appoint judges which are expert in coursing and shall stand on the hillside whither they perceive the hare will bend, to mark which dog doeth best and to give judgement thereof accordingly: some use when their Greyhounds be both of a colour, to bind a handkerchief about one of their necks for a difference.'

In time the National Coursing Club was established in 1858, following a series of successful events including the first Waterloo Cup Meeting, held as an eight-dog stake in 1836 at Altcar in Liverpool.

The Greyhound Stud Book was opened in 1882 and, to this day, all hounds must be entered if they are to enter any of Britain's recognized coursing matches. It was during the 19th century that enclosed areas were introduced for coursing. The hare would be released at one end of the ground and the Greyhounds were expected to catch it before it reached the escape hole at the far end. This type of coursing is now illegal in Britain, although it is still practised in some other parts of the world. The present rules of the National Coursing Club, which are similar to those of Australia, Spain and some other countries, allow for heats in which two dogs compete against each other. Each heat starts with the brace of dogs being put into contraptions called slips, special collars joined together by a long lead and a mechanical opening device. A trained handler, known as the slipper, walks the two competing dogs ahead of the field of spectators which spread in a long straight line on either side. When a hare gets up, the dogs become very excited, but the slipper must allow the quarry to get about 82 yards (75 m) away before the dogs are simultaneously released by a pull on the handle which opens the slips.

Greyhound Racing

The sport of Greyhound racing quite naturally evolved from coursing, although it was only after a period of many years that it became really popular. A report in *The Times* newspaper, dated 11 September 1876, shows that a form of racing, with hounds chasing after a mechanical hare, took place in Hendon, Middlesex, behind an inn called the Welsh Harp. At this meeting several races were run over a distance of 400 yards (366 m), along which a grooved track had been specially laid to carry an artificial hare, pulled by a rope attached to a windlass. Coursing enthusiasts were very opposed to this new sport and it was left to the Americans to devise and develop dog-racing in an organized manner.

From 1874 in the U.S.A. dogs were raced on horse-race tracks. Then, in 1909, the first official Greyhound track opened with a first-class meeting in Tucson, Arizona. The first British track was opened in Manchester on 24 July 1926 and an excited crowd of more than 2000 spectators saw 'Mistley', a Greyhound with only half a tail, win the opening race. On 1 January 1928 the British National Greyhound Racing Club was formed and instituted stringent rules for registration of Greyhounds and the organization of their racing.

Today, Greyhound racing has become a very popular sport in Britain, North America, Australia and many other countries of the world, and although it is sometimes termed the working-man's racing, events are attended and enjoyed by folks from all walks of life.

Although it is not necessary to be very rich in order to enjoy the ownership of a racing Greyhound, the costs of keeping such a dog in training can be quite substantial. A suitable puppy is purchased and very carefully reared, being fed a correctly balanced diet and given just the right sort of exercise. When old enough, the puppy is passed to a licensed trainer to learn how to chase after a mechanical hare. At 15 months of age, the young dog is still classed as a puppy for racing purposes, but if it shows aptitude during preliminary trials, it is then entitled to race in public.

The dog racetrack is oval in shape. Immediately inside the perimeter rails an imitation hare is electrically propelled at a regulated speed, being affixed to a metal arm attached to a moving trolley. Most races have six starters which are put into special stalls by their handlers. The dogs are muzzled and are trained to this procedure from an early age. The stalls or traps are fitted with quick-release electrically operated doors which simultaneously open at the touch of the starter's button, and the Greyhounds burst out and into their racing stride. Most races are over a distance of 500 yards, but a meeting may have an eight-race card or a mixed programme of events, including sprints, hurdles and staying races over distances from 400 to 1156 yards (366 to 1057 m). The Greyhounds move at seemingly breathtaking speeds, and may achieve an astonishing average speed of about 38 mph (61 km/h).

Greyhound racing has become a big commercial enterprise in many countries of the world. In Spain, for example, it competes with the more traditional bull-fight as a major spectator sport, and with top-quality dogs imported from Britain, Ireland and the United States of America, the standard is very high. In Australia and Tasmania Greyhound racing reached peak popularity in 1960, thanks to government sponsorship and the awarding of big money prizes to the winning dogs. The leading meetings, such as the Australian Cup, draw vast crowds and attract the best Greyhounds, ensuring good sport for all. In the Far East dog-racing is popular too, and bets are placed on likely Greyhounds in Hong Kong, Macao and Malaysia. In Indonesia the Djakarta track is immensely popular, while on the other side of the world, in Florida, the sport ranks number one with mil-

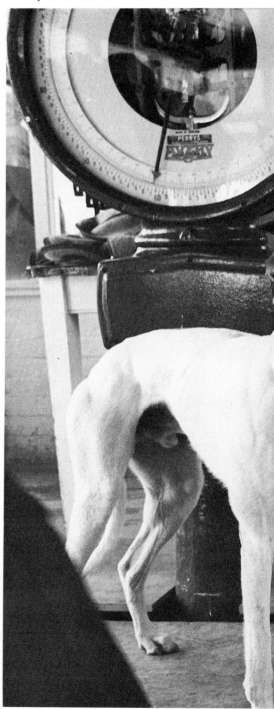

lions of people attending the meetings and millions of dollars being won and lost.

Commercial Greyhounds live pampered lives, but do not enjoy the companionship and comforts of a home environment. A dog will be in racing condition for about three years, during which time it receives the very best of food, housing and training. Usually looked after by a kennel girl, the dog is regularly groomed and kept clean and warm. On race day, a strict routine is observed and the dog will be let out early then given a light breakfast of milk and cereal. A restful morning is followed by a small and carefully formulated lunch. Then the dog is quietly exercised at the walk before being given a thorough grooming to clean the coat and tone up all the muscles. The dog must be transported to the track, arriving one hour before the start of the first race, and then has to submit to stringent tests. A gas chromatography test of urine sample is made to detect the possible presence of any drugs in the bloodstream and ten minutes before its race, the dog is given a veterinary check and is weighed in. The veterinary surgeon looks for any sign of lameness or illness, and bitches are checked to ensure that they are not in oestrus. At the end of racing, a further veterinary check is given before the dog is allowed to return home to the trainer's kennels. Then it is rubbed down and given a

Racing greyhounds are meticulously checked and weighed before and after each competitive run.

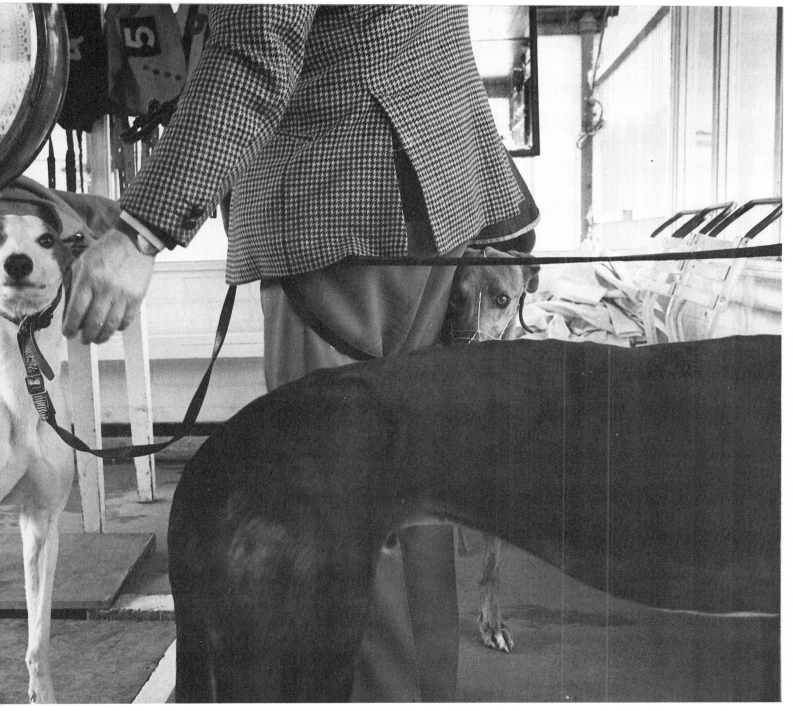

A group of splendid Salukis. The breed is extremely old, and was well known in Ancient Egypt.

good feed before being left to rest through the night.

Thousands of Greyhounds are bred for the racing industry, but only about 75 per cent of the puppies are found to be of desired conformation, fast enough or of a suitable temperament. The remainder are discarded in the first 18 months. Over half of the 75 per cent are also discarded due to injury or problems in training, faulty stamina or lack of necessary speed, and the balance settle down to the job of racing. Discarded Greyhounds may be humanely destroyed, sold to research laboratories or passed on to pet homes. There are several societies which help in homing and rehabilitation of young discarded Greyhounds and older retired racing dogs, but unfortunately, the supply of animals generally seems to outweigh the supply of suitable homes. Very successful Greyhounds are, of course, in demand as stud dogs and brood bitches.

Whippets

Rather like a small Greyhound in appearance is another coursing breed known as the Whippet, first bred in the Midlands and Northern counties of England about a century ago, for rabbiting and coursing. The Whippet or 'poor man's Greyhound' was commonly used for rabbit coursing matches in which wild rabbits were netted and set free in an enclosed area in front of pairs of dogs held by the official slipper. Although the quarry was given about 60 yards (55 m) start, there was no chance of escape and the winner of each heat was the dog which first reached and snapped up the prey. Criticism of the cruelty involved in this 'sport' caused its discontinuance and attention was then turned to the racing of these small hounds along a straight grass or cinder track. Speed was of the utmost importance. The dogs were carefully bred, fed and trained, and were officially handicapped according

Speed is essential when leaving the traps, for it is here that valuable ground may be gained – or lost!

to their size and sex, bitches being generally faster than dogs. Hard-working miners in their off-duty hours from the coal-face would enjoy placing small wagers on the results of rag-races. The little dogs were trained to race as fast as they could to the 'rag', usually a scarf or neckerchief being waved by its handler at the finish line. At the start of a rag-race, the dogs, each weighing around 17 lb (8 kg) were held by individual slippers, with one hand on the scruff of the animal's neck and the other hand grasping the base of the tail. The owner or trainer then showed the dog its 'rag' and ran down the track to the winning line. At the sound of the starting pistol, each slipper would hurl his dog forward into a flying start, and the Whippet would then race the 200 yards (183 m) to its owner who was frantically waving the 'rag'. Past the winning line each dog leaped at his respective 'rag' hanging on with gripping jaws. Rag racing was particularly popular in Lancashire, and at both Oldham and Bury it was not unusual for 300 or more dogs to be entered in one handicap. Puppies were trained from an early age, always being called to their food or for a game or reward by the waving of a rag.

Other Racing and Coursing Dogs

Throughout Europe owners of other types of hounds enjoy racing their dogs through their local clubs and societies. There are strict racing rules, but even so the participants enjoy a high level of sport. Although Greyhound racing takes pride of place in most Scandinavian countries, there is no betting and only trophies are given as prizes. This has kept the sport on a friendly amateur-style basis, and has allowed, also, the staging of Cup meetings for the racing of Whippets, Afghan Hounds and Salukis.

The **Saluki** is a very ancient breed, well known in Ancient Egyptian times. Carvings and paintings dating as far back as 5000 B.C. show dogs exactly like the present-day Saluki, and the alternative spellings of Saluqi and Slughi mean 'hound' and today's **Sloughi** is another Greyhound type, rather like a short-coated Saluki. Egyptologists consider that the Saluki may be traced back to a very ancient race of dogs and it is referred to in an ancient Arab poem, well over 1000 years old, which has the line 'My dog brought by Kings from Saluk'. It is quite true to say that the Saluki has

been used to course gazelles and hares in the desert from the days of the Pharaohs. It is still used for the same purpose to this day and is sometimes worked in conjunction with falcons. To the Arab, all animals are unclean, but he does not consider the Saluki to be a dog – he treats it like his favourite horse considering it to be a most precious possession entitled to share his tent, his food and his life. In some Arabic writings the Saluki is described by the author as 'my butcher'. One man, being entertained by a sheikh, politely enquired how it was that the meal could consist of game caught and killed by a dog, and was gently reminded that the Saluki was not a dog but a hound. Salukis were never sold by their Arab masters, but were occasionally given as gifts to honoured guests. It was in this way that the breed gradually spread and became popular throughout the world.

Afghan Hounds look very similar to Salukis, apart from the tail which is set rather high and curls upwards at the tip. Rock carvings in Balkh, situated in northwest Afghanistan, are dated at 2000 B.C. and indicate the extreme antiquity of the breed. It is possible that both the Saluki and the Afghan Hound may be traced to a common ancestor, or that one has descended from the other, but whatever its origin, it is true to say that the Afghan is an efficient hunting dog ideally suited to the difficult terrain of the land of its birth. The protective coat, shaggy and tough in its natural state, keeps out the cold and saves the skin from damage as it works among

the craggy rocks and thorny bushes of its homeland. The natural quarry of the Afghan over the years has included the wolf, leopard and wild boar as well as hare, fox, jackal and antelope, and the hound has always been favoured as a fine guard-dog as well as an intrepid hunter.

It was in 1895 that the first pair of Afghan Barukzy Hounds were exhibited at the old Royal Aquarium in London, but little headway was made in the development of the breed until Captain John Barff imported a sensational dog called 'Zardin' in 1907, very well made and sound with perfect action and a full coat of a true rich red colour. With more imports and the dedication of a few keen breeders the Afghan was established in Britain and received official Kennel Club recognition in 1926.

Overleaf: An Afghan Hound at full gallop.

Below: The Saluki has always proved a popular participant in hare-coursing contests.

Hounds

The ancient Greeks valued dogs for hunting and their passion for the chase was such that stories of hounds and hunting feature prominently in the myths and legends of those times. In the *Odyssey*, written about 850 B.C., a moving passage tells of how Odysseus returns in disguise to his home after an absence of many years and sees his old hound, 'Argus', lying below the city gates. As a young man Odysseus had taken the hound hunting for wild goat, deer and hare, but having been left behind and virtually abandoned, for so long, the old animal now lay on a dung heap, at the point of death and ridden with vermin. As his master approached and was recognized, the old dog raised his head, dropped his ears and feebly wagged his tail. Odysseus saw the dog, and brushing tears from his eyes said to his companion 'Eumaeus, it is very odd to see a hound like this lying in the dung. He is a beauty, though one cannot tell whether his looks were matched by his

Left: A Roman statue showing small dogs of greyhound type tenaciously tackling a large stag.

Above: This mosaic shows a much larger, massively built hound about to tackle a wild boar. Museo Comunale, Rome.

pace, or whether he was just one of those dogs whom their masters feed at table and keep for show. . .' His friend recognizing the faithful 'Argus' replied 'No game to which he gave chase could escape him in the forest glades, for besides all he was a marvel at picking up the scent.' 'Argus' was too old to lift himself to greet his returned master, and the effort of welcome was too much for his tired heart. It was as though he had kept himself alive for the return of Odysseus, and having seen him once again slipped quietly into death.

As the passage shows, the powers of speed and scent in the dog were more highly esteemed than beauty, and in his later years, Xenophon, the great Athenian mercenary and writer, retired to Elis, to breed hunting dogs.

From his experiences in this field he wrote his book *Cyngeticus*, in which he discussed two quite distinct breeds of hounds, the substantial Castorian and the fox-like Alopecide.

Xenophon criticized breeders who produced inferior dogs, and considered that a perfect hound should be large, deep-chested and well-muscled, with a small head, square muzzle and deep stop, wrinkled forehead, thin ears and bright, black eyes. He fully described the Hound of Sparta, known as the Laconian, and considered it to be the most prized of all Greek hounds. Light but strongly built, the Laconian was possessed of amazing scenting powers and was employed at the beginning of the hunt to pick up the scent of wild boar and to trace the whereabouts of the quarry. Once this

Above: Hunting dogs were often unpredictable and vicious and could not be trusted with strangers. Museo Civico, Palermo.

White Talbot hounds pulling down a wild boar.

had descended from wolves, foxes and jackals and described their processes of reproduction. Greek hounds were notoriously fierce and unpredictable, probably due to a high proportion of feral blood, and sometimes turned on their masters. Euripides, the Greek playwright and satirist, was tragically killed by a hound while staying at the court of King Archelaus of Macedonia. Theocritus, the romantic Greek poet, aware of such dangers, wrote of a young shepherd girl playing in the sea, watched by a hound 'Take heed that he leap not upon the maiden's limbs as she rises from the salt water, see that he rend not her lovely body.'

Most of today's British and European hounds are believed to have descended from a pack founded in the Ardennes during the 7th and 8th centuries. François Hubert, son of Bertrand, Duc de Guienne, was a keen huntsman and bred his own strain of distinctive hounds. After the death of his beloved wife, Floribane, the grief-stricken François was out with his hounds on Good Friday when he had a vision, and saw before him a huge stag, carrying a glowing golden cross in its branching antlers. Very affected by his experience, François Hubert entered a monastery, but continued breeding his special hounds. One hundred years after his death, the monk was canonized, and his hounds also took his new name of Saint Hubert. Successive abbots and monks continued with the careful, selective breeding of the Bloodhounds, which were noted for their endurance, courage and scenting abilities. Two main groups had emerged, the true black **St. Hubert Hounds** and the larger white **Talbot Hounds**, named after Taillebois, François Hubert's successor. St. Hubert's Day is remembered each year on 3 November by a traditional blessing ceremony of the hounds which takes place in the Little Chapel of St. Hubert, built in 1610 at Tervueren, near Brussels. Other similar hound-blessing ceremonies are carried out before each hunting season in France and Belgium, and in Ireland all hounds are blessed on the day reserved as the Feast of St. Hubert.

William the Conqueror brought his packs of St. Hubert Hounds to Britain after the Norman Conquest of 1066. The Normans and the Plantagenets were all fond of hunting with 'scent' hounds and many packs of Bloodhounds were retained for hunting stag.

was done, the precious hound was taken off the line and a mixed pack of fighting hounds was loosed to run down the boar and effect the kill. The mixed pack would have included Indian, Cretan and Locrian dogs, some of which were of the Mastiff type, brought to Greece by Xerxes, the invading King of Persia, in 480 B.C. This form of hunting, using specialized dogs for different stages of the chase, was to continue for at least 1000 years.

Aristotle, the great Greek scholar who lived from 384–322 B.C., was a gifted naturalist and among his many works is *Historia Animalium*, an introduction to biology, in which he discusses the evolution and classification of animals. He considered that dogs

William Rufus hunted with his Blood-hounds in the vast tracts of the New Forest, and both Henry III and Henry IV drew up strict rules for the keeping and training of their prized personal packs.

Edward, Duke of York, produced his treatise, *Master of Game*, in the 15th century, and talking of hounds wrote: 'A hound is of great understanding and of great knowledge, a hound hath great strength and great goodness.' He described the special Dog Boys, kept to live with and care for the hounds: 'Also I will teach the child to lead out the hounds to scombre twice in a day ... and he shall lead them into some fair place where tender grass grows as corn and other things, that therewith may they feed themselves as it is med-icine for them.' He advocated roomy, sunny kennels, with a loft above to keep them warm in winter and cool in summer, and a well-drained grassy area on which the hounds could exer-cise and play.

Bloodhounds

Bloodhounds are the oldest of all hound types and throughout their long and varied history have retained one special characteristic, that of the ability to follow a cold, old scent. They have always been very large and rather slow workers but possessed of unequalled powers of concentration, patience and perseverance. A hound with pendulous ears, closely resem-bling a Bloodhound, is etched on a Babylonian terra-cotta tablet, dated at about 2000 B.C., and other records show similar hounds with some evi-dence of Mastiff blood being used as war dogs in ancient Mesopotamia.

Stag hunting with a mixed pack of white and coloured hounds in France. Bibliothèque Nationale, Paris.

The name, Bloodhound, was given to the breed as they had all descended from one pure bloodline; it has nothing whatsoever to do with the following of a blood-trail. These hounds have been called several other names through the centuries, including: Limier, Lymo-Ho and Lymer, because they were frequently worked on a lyam or long tracking leash; Sleuth or Sleuth Hounds; Slot or Slough Hounds – a 'slot' being the footprint of a deer, and 'to slot' meaning to track deer.

From about 1200 onwards it was traditional to send three couples of St. Hubert's Hounds from their monastery kennels as a gift to the King of France. The hounds were greatly prized and the French King, in turn, sent some as a gift to Queen Elizabeth I of England.

In Mediaeval times most monasteries kept their own packs of hounds and bishops and other church dignitaries enjoyed their hunting days. Although the Bloodhounds of those times were the prized possessions of the clergy and the aristocracy, commoners did enjoy both the sight and sounds of such hounds at work.

It was in the 16th and 17th centuries that the amazing scenting powers of Bloodhounds were first employed to hunt men, generally poachers and sheep stealers, but also the wounded who had escaped from the battlefield. After the death of the English King Charles II, the Duke of Monmouth, claimant to the throne, met the armies of James II at Sedgemoor in the West Country. As darkness fell on the night

of 5 July 1685, heavy mists hampered his men, and they blundered into the deep watercourses of the area. Much of Monmouth's ammunition failed, and as dawn broke, his men were ruthlessly cut down in a fierce and bloody battle. The severely wounded Duke managed to escape and hid himself for several days. He was eventually sought out by a pack of the King's Bloodhounds who found him at the point of death, concealed in a waterlogged ditch. A fine horseman and a great lover of horses and hounds it was an unfair fate for a brave man, for despite a pitiable personal interview with the King, the unfortunate Duke was mercilessly executed.

As time went by, Bloodhounds were used less for hunting and more for quelling riots and tracking down men, and careful crosses were made with other dogs to introduce savage tendencies without losing the unique scenting powers. Some crosses were made which produced hounds for other purposes, the Staghounds, for instance, and the famous Kerry Beagles both have a proportion of Bloodhound ancestry.

It is likely that the **Staghound** has now ceased to exist as a separate breed, although the hunting of stags still takes place. The Royal Kennels at Windsor kept a pack of specialized Staghounds until the early part of the 19th century, and these were described as being up to 30 inches (76 cm) at

Above: 'Barnaby' and 'Burgho', two renowned bloodhounds employed to hunt the infamous Jack the Ripper.

Left: Nose-down, this hound is onto a strong, distinctive trail, enabling it to track at high speed.

Right: Modern working bloodhounds.

the shoulder and mostly white in colour. Because of this it can be assumed that they are almost pure descendants of the old Talbot Hounds. Said to be very strong, fast and persistent, the Staghound has such perceptive scenting powers that it was able to track an individual deer through a whole herd. The Windsor Staghounds were exported as an entire pack to France, where they were undoubtedly used in the production of other hound varieties.

The **Kerry Beagle** is misnamed for it is a hound that bears no resemblance whatsoever to any of the Beagle family. The Kerry looks like a light and rather leggy Bloodhound, black and tan in colour and is limited to one pack now, in Southern Ireland. Exports were made to the United States in the 19th century and it is quite possible that the Kerry was used in the production of the American Foxhound and the Black and Tan Coonhound, a comparatively new breed first officially recognized in 1945.

In the 19th century Bloodhounds were trained to track sheep stealers and public displays of the hounds' prowess were sometimes given. In America Bloodhounds were prized for their superb scenting abilities, and one famous animal, called 'Nick Carter',

was responsible for over 600 arrests. Stories of hounds' exploits made the record books, and one famous hound followed a trail that was 105 hours cold, over a distance of 50 miles (80 km), but this was beaten in 1954 when hounds belonging to Mr. Norman Wilson, found the body of a child who had been missing for 13 days and ten hours.

Dog Shows began in Britain in 1859 and soon became a fashionable pastime. *The Dogs of the British Isles* was written in 1886 by Mr. J. H. Walsh, one of the first official dog-show judges, and contains some fascinating observations of breeds at that time. In his section on the Bloodhound he describes it as being a large and mostly uncontrollable animal with a very independent character.

The Bloodhound of today is kept in Britain mainly as a show dog or as a family pet, but there is also an exciting sport organized especially for the breed in which the hounds are able to show off their skills in tracking. Working trials for Bloodhounds are held under Kennel Club rules. Each animal works separately and is judged on its individual performance. The Bloodhound must be specially trained for trials work and is fitted with a special harness which enables it to get its head down low enough to follow a line of scent. The trainer follows behind holding the end of a trail leash which is about 40 ft (13 m) long. Puppies as young as seven weeks show signs of following trails and preliminary training can begin. When serious training commences at around eight or nine months of age, the Bloodhound puppy is able to follow quite cold trails over all sorts of terrain, and as it becomes more experienced the young dog is introduced to difficult weather conditions and lines laid through flocks of sheep, poultry yards and fields of cattle. Bloodhounds are not now used for tracking down criminals in Britain but the practice still continues with great success in the United States of America, as well as in certain other countries.

Basset Hounds

The Basset is a very old breed, originally developed to hunt wild boar, deer and wolves particularly in France where 'bas' means low or dwarfed. There are several varieties, rough-coated, smooth-coated, straight-legged and those with crooked legs, but all have distinct Bloodhound characteristics in head shape, bell-like voices and strong scenting abilities.

At the first dog show held in Paris in 1863, several English visitors had the opportunity of seeing the breed for the first time, and in 1866 a pair of hounds were presented by the Marquis of Tourman to Lord Galway. The breed was first popularized as a show dog, but was eventually put to work hunting the hare in 1844. Being rather slow and methodical in their work, Basset Hounds have never achieved the same popularity as the Beagle, but their distinctive 'music' is a sound never to be forgotten.

Beagles

In his *Cynegeticus* Xenophon described the hunting of the hare using very small hounds which sound very like the Beagles of today. The Romans quite probably carried some of these useful little hounds with them to Britain and by the reign of King Canute, 'certain smalle houndes' were exempted from the forest laws codified in 1016. The first use of the name, 'Beagle', seems to have occurred *circa* 1481, and by the reign of Elizabeth I, the name was in common usage for the Tudor queen kept an entire pack of diminutive hounds referred to as the 'Singing Beagles'. Royalty seemed to favour the neat hounds, for William of Orange kept a pack, and in the early 19th century, George IV hunted with his Beagles regularly over the Sussex Downs and posed for a court painting with his pack arranged around his feet. Type was very variable within the breed, but the sort aimed for was a

This Basset hound appears to have lost the scent of his quarry at the river bank.

miniature version of the old Southern Hound, almost certainly descended from the Talbot.

In his *History of Quadrupeds*, first published in 1790, Thomas Bewick's engraving of a Beagle shows it to be a fine looking, streamlined type of hound, with a very well-proportioned body and a strong head. It was obviously popular and in the succeeding century, efforts were made to standardize its type. In 1890 the Beagle Club was formed and held its first show in 1896, giving owners the chance to meet, compare and match their hounds. Today, Beagles are still worked in packs by huntsmen on foot, and have also found niches for themselves in the show world and as family house pets.

Foxhounds

Although there are records of the hunting of foxes going back to the 13th century, the earliest pack of hounds used exclusively for fox-hunting was the Charlton in Sussex, formed about the year 1688. The original Foxhounds were said to have been bred from crosses between the Northern Hounds, which were most probably rough-coated Deerhounds, and the Southern Hounds of Talbot descent. Later on some Greyhound blood was added to give greater speed, then each hunt settled down to practise the selective breeding techniques which have

resulted in the standardized **English Foxhound** of today. Some variation is still seen between hounds of different packs, for the great variation in types of countryside call for slightly different characteristics in the hounds. Some packs are bred to specific colour standards, one pack having all black and tan hounds for example, while the hounds of another pack may be predominantly white with light markings. Hounds used in thickly wooded country need to be short and stocky and able to stick to the line, while in areas of wide open grassed countryside,

hounds must be fast and full of stamina. In Britain's Fell country, hounds must be able to scramble over rocks and be immune to hostile weather conditions, while the light-coloured hounds of Wales are rough-coated and easily seen as they clamber among the hills and coombs.

Some packs of Foxhounds have records going back to the beginning of the 18th century, showing purchases of hounds and exchanges of breeding stock with other packs. The Master of Foxhounds Association opened its stud book in 1880 and, at that time,

there were listed 140 packs throughout Britain. When Robert Brooke sailed to America in 1650 he took with him his own pack of hounds, the descendants of which were destined to remain with his family for the following 300 or more years. Further imports of hound stock were purchased from Britain and France during the 18th century and also from Ireland in the 19th century.

In the United States of America the **American Foxhound** is used for four quite different purposes, and, therefore, four different types of hound have been developed. The field trial hound must run competitively in speed trials; a slower hound with a good voice is necessary for those who hunt the fox with a gun; trail or drag hounds are used to follow a man-laid drag line; and finally there is pack-hunting, popular in Virginia, where a hound similar to the English Foxhound is required, combining speed, stamina, a good voice and a natural tendency to pack together.

Other Hounds

The **Harrier** looks rather like a small Foxhound, but it is a separate breed. The Penistone was the first pack of Harriers in Britain and was established in 1260 by Sir Elias de Midhope. It then hunted regularly for more than five hundred years. Harriers in Britain are used mainly for hunting the hare on foot, though they may occasionally be asked to hunt foxes. In the United States where they have been worked since colonial times, Harriers have found favour for drag hunting in recent years.

The **Otterhound** looks very like a rough-coated Bloodhound in appearance and is a very old and rare breed. Both Henry II and Queen Elizabeth I had their own packs. Today otters are very scarce and the few remaining packs of Otterhounds are often used to hunt feral mink menacing the game fish in peaceful river stretches as well as providing useful information to help keep track of the otters.

Above: Young riders wait patiently while hounds search for the fox's scent.

Right: Otterhounds working a riverbank.

Terriers

Terriers, after the Hound group, are the best known of all hunting dogs, and come in a wide range of shapes, sizes, colours and coat types. The name, 'terrier', comes from the French word *terrier* derived from Low-Latin *Terracium*, which, in turn, comes from the Latin *terra*, meaning earth. There are reports from the year 54 B.C., that the invading Roman soldiers of Julius Caesar, having established themselves in their garrisons on British soil, saw 'strange-appearing dogs which followed their quarry into the ground'.

One of the earliest written descriptions of the terrier is found in a treatise on *English Dogs*, written by Dr. Johannes Caius, physician to Queen Elizabeth I and founder of Caius Col-

lege, Cambridge. The work was produced for inclusion in the *Historic Animalium*, by Konrad von Gesner, published in 1553, and later translated back into English by Abraham Fleming in 1576. Caius talks of 'Terrarius' or 'Terrars' as being 'dogges serving y pastime of hunting beasts' and an extract from the work reads: 'Another sort of hunting dog there is which hunteth the Foxe and Badger or Greye only, whom we call Terrars because they (after the manner and custom of ferrets in searching after Conneyes) creepe into the ground and by that means make afrayde, nyppe and byte the Fox and the Badger in such sort, that eyther they teare them in pieces with thyr teeth being in the bosom of

Opposite page, top: 'Terriers Ratting' by George Armfield. 1840–1875. National Gallery of British Sports and Pastimes.

Opposite page, bottom: Hounds and hunt terriers find and finish a fox.

Below: This early 19th century engraving by Henry Alken shows several contemporary dog breeds including some early bull-terriers.

the earth, or else hayle and pull them perforce out of their lurking angles, darke dongeons and close caves, or at least through conceded feare drive them out of their follow harbours, in so much that they are compelled to prepare speedie flyte, and being desirous of the next (albeit not the safest) refuge, are otherwise taken and trapped with snares and nettes layde over holes to the same purpose.'

Even earlier, Dame Juliana Berners' *Boke of St. Albans* of 1466, describes 'teroures', and mentions that they had both rough and smooth coats, but it is impossible to recognize any of today's specific breeds from her work. Terriers were obviously bred for various sorts of hunting, and were selected for their ability rather than their looks. Then, as specific types showed particular aptitude for certain game, or an improved performance over difficult terrain, it was selectively bred to fix those desired characteristics. The first indication of such selection was given by Turbeville, a contemporary of Dr. Caius, in his translation of the work of Du Foulloux, on the entering of terriers: 'You must understand that there are sundrie sortes of Terryers whereof we hold opinion that one sorte came out of Flaunders or the Low Countries, as Artoys and thereabouts and they have crooked legges, and are shorte heared moste commonly. Another sorte there is which are shagged and straight legged: those with the crooked legges wyll take earth better than the other, and are better for the Badgerd, bycause they will lye longer at a vermine: but the others with streyght legges do serve for two purposes, for they wyll Hunte above the grounde as well as do other houndes, and will enter the earthe with more furie than the others: but they wyll not abide so long, bycause they are too eagre in fight, and therefore are constreyned to come out to take the ayre: there are both good and badde of bothe sortes.' Though the original French version of this work uses the term 'basset' this is from 'bas' the French word for low, and other works of the time talk of basset-terriers. What is certain is that short-legged dogs of the Dachshund type were found very useful for going to earth after their prey, while the taller types were better able to run with the pack of hounds. Today's hunt terriers are very game and quite fearless, but being very small, are often carried for long distances by the huntsmen, on the pommels of their saddles.

A terrier's best colour depended to a great extent on the type of work it was expected to do, for it was often important for the huntsman to be able to see the little dog working among bracken, rocks or reeds. It was also important that gamekeepers and other hunters could readily distinguish between the dogs and foxes or other small animals. Peter Beckford in his classic *Thoughts on Hunting* of 1781 makes this point clear: 'You should always keep a terrier in at the fox; for if you do not, he not only may move, but also in loose ground may dig himself in. . . . I should prefer a black or white terrier: some are so like the fox that awkward people frequently mistake one for the other. If you like terriers to run with your pack, large ones, at times, are useful; but in an earth they do little good as they cannot always get up to a fox.' Here we see that both black and white terriers were known as that time, as well as those so rufous that they might be mistaken for foxes. We also know from other records that the terriers of those days wore collars hung with bells to encourage the foxes and badgers to start from their tunnels.

The Reverend W. B. Daniel was opposed to the sport of badger-baiting, but considered hunting essential for the control of vermin. His book of 1801 makes several interesting comments regarding terriers, their temperament, size, shape and colour: 'No species of dogs will fight the badger so resolutely and fairly as terriers of which there are two kinds, the one is rough, short-legged, long-backed, very strong and most commonly of a black or yellowish colour mixt with white; the other is smooth-haired and beautifully formed, having a shorter body and more sprightly appearance; is generally of a reddish-brown colour or black with tan legs; both are the determined foe of all the vermin kind. . . . The black or red-and-white are to be preferred, those that are altogether of a reddish colour awkward people may mistake for a fox.'

In 1834 a magazine article on terriers described the group as consisting of two breeds: the rough-haired **Scottish Terrier** and the smooth-haired **English Terrier**. The former was about 12 inches (30 cm) high, with a muscular body and sturdy legs. The proportionately large head had a pointed muzzle and small, half-pricked ears. Its true colours were either sandy or black, and although some white or pied dogs were about, these were considered less hardy and of inpure breeding. The Scottish Terrier was further divided into three varieties, the first exactly as described above and with a longish, hard coat. The second variety, found mostly in the western islands of Scotland, had a longer, somewhat flowing coat, while the third was about 3 inches (8 cm) taller, and with a very short hard and wiry coat. A note stated that it was from this third type that some of the best Bull Terriers were obtained.

The English Terrier was described as being a handsome, sprightly dog generally black on the top of the head, the neck, back, sides, top and tail, while the belly and throat were bright reddish-brown. This dog had a small head with a nose of medium length, and small, erect ears. It stood between 10 and 18 inches (25 and 46 cm) high.

This typical black-and-tan coat pattern is considered by zoologists and geneticists to be a primitive form, probably inherent in all breeds, and several modern-day dogs exhibit this characteristic.

Black-and-tan terrier breeds of today include the Airedale, the Lakeland, the Norfolk, the Norwich and the Welsh, all of which have hard, wiry coats. The smooth coated Manchester Terrier, however, is merely a refined version of the old Black-and-Tan Terrier, famous for its skill in killing rats and in coursing rabbits. It was to

Above: In terrier racing, traps are used to ensure a fair start.

Top: A perky Cairn Terrier working happily in the undergrowth.

Right: Several types of terriers are shown in this interesting print made in 1820.

Opposite page: This engraving shows a terrier in competition in a New Jersey rat pit during the last century.

increase the dogs' speed for this last sport that some Whippet blood was introduced, producing the type and style now seen in the Manchester Terrier of today.

It is most probable that the old Black-and-Tan Terriers were crossed with the Bulldogs of the early 19th century and from the unions were produced efficient fighting dogs, the ancestors of today's **Staffordshire Bull Terriers**. These dogs were very agile, with tremendous strength of jaw, immense courage and an insatiable desire to fight. Although indisputably ugly, they became one of the most popular of sporting dogs, especially among undergraduates and young men of the last century. Dog fights were quite ritualistic, and special fighting pits were constructed in the yards of public houses and inns. The rules were simple, and the pits were rectangular with boarded sides, so that crowds of spectators could watch in safety. Wagers were placed on the outcome of the matches, and sometimes a great deal of money would be placed on a famous dog. The object of the fight was not so much the ability to kill the opposing dog but for the animal to be game enough to make the attempt. A 'scratch' line was drawn across the centre of the pit and the two dogs to be matched were held by their handlers or 'setters' at opposite ends of the pit. Each dog was released in turn and encouraged to cross the line

to attack the other. The battle was lost by the first dog that failed to 'come up to scratch'.

The Humane Act of 1835 was introduced to stop such cruel sports as bear-baiting and bull-baiting, as well as abolishing dog-fighting, but although the baitings ceased, organized dog-fights continued more or less openly, for several years. The old Pit Bull Terrier was taken by famous Birmingham dog dealer James Hicks in 1860 and crossed with the now extinct Old English White Terrier, to produce a strain of all-white dogs renowned for their ratting abilities and complete fearlessness. Today the refined descendants of these dogs are known as English **Bull Terriers**.

Today's Terrier Breeds

Today most people's idea of a true terrier is the popular **Wire Fox Terrier**, well known as a top winning show dog, with its alert carriage and neatly trimmed coat. Both this and its close cousin the **Smooth Fox Terrier** are descended from dogs that used to run with packs of Foxhounds in the last century.

Despite its popularity though, the Fox Terrier must concede place to the great **Airedale** for the title, King of Terriers. This breed originated in the valley of the River Aire in Yorkshire, and resulted from crosses between the old Black-and-Tan Terrier and either Otterhounds or Welsh Harriers. The

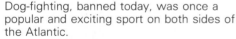

Dog-fighting, banned today, was once a popular and exciting sport on both sides of the Atlantic.

PREPARING FOR THE FRAY.

CATCHING THE RATS.

THE SCENE AT THE PIT.

TONER'S "BLANCHE"

JEFF CARPENTER'S TERRIER.

large terriers that resulted were first called Waterside Terriers, then Bingley Terriers and were valued for their hunting abilities along the river banks catching otters, voles, rats and rabbits. As a bonus the breed was found to have a very strong guarding instinct, and to be extremely reliable with small children. By 1884 the breed was classified as the Airedale Terrier by the British Kennel Club and exports were made from Britain to all parts of the world. In France they hunted wild boar, in Africa waterbuck and bushbuck, and in America they became police dogs – an Airedale won the first Police Dog Trials held in New York's Madison Square Garden. The breed's intelligence and 'trainability' came to the fore in the First World War when Airedales were used as war dogs, car-rying vital messages across minefields, and testing difficult terrain.

The **Irish Terrier** is a smart red dog, smaller and racier than the Airedale, but built on similar lines. Nicknamed the 'daredevil' it is an excellent ratter, and has been used with success in the shooting field.

Two other large Irish breeds of terrier are the **Soft-coated Wheaten** and its descendant, the **Kerry Blue**. Both have similar soft, waved silky coats, but while the blue-coated Kerry Blue is trimmed for showing, the honey-coloured Wheaten is left as nature intended. Both breeds were developed as all-round farm dogs, good at killing vermin and guarding the home. The Kerry is a good cattle dog, and the Wheaten has been successfully trained as a gundog.

Opposite page: The Bull Terrier remains a trusted and fearless companion to this day.

The Smooth Fox Terrier's type has remained very similar to that of his forebears.

The **Lakeland Terrier** looks very like a miniature Airedale and was bred for hunting foxes with the Lakeland packs. These hounds are worked on foot as the terrain is too rocky for horsemen. The terrier is expected to flush foxes from the rocky outcrops or 'borrans' or to make the kill if the fox is cornered in an inaccessible place. The **Welsh Terrier** is sometimes confused with the Lakeland, but is a much older breed, and has been used in packs in the Welsh hills for hunting foxes. Another Welsh breed is the **Sealyham**, named after the estate of its founder, Captain John Edwardes, who first bred the unusual little white dogs for badger-digging in 1840. Also white but of totally different type and

character, is the **West Highland White**, one of the terrier breeds from Scotland, and closely related to the **Cairn Terrier**. Both breeds are tough and agile and were always valued for their work and hunting ability. The Cairn was so called because of its ability to bolt foxes and otters from the rocky cairns of its homeland. The true Scottish Terrier is a keen worker and makes a good family guard, and whereas the Cairn is red, sandy, grey or brindled, the 'Scottie' is generally black, although the brindled is also a recognized colour. The **Dandie Dinmont** was bred for working underground and its soft dark eyes belie a tough, fierce and workmanlike character. Pepper or mustard in colour,

The Sealyham Terrier was first bred for badger hunting in 1840.

Border Terriers are game and plucky dogs, excellent workers and kind with children.

Above: The West Highland White has evolved as a popular family pet as well as a perfect country companion.

Right: The Jack Russell terrier is at home in almost any situation.

Left: First bred in Sydney, Australia, the Silky terrier is descended from several other small dogs including the diminutive 'Yorkie'.

Below: This is 'Rats', a cross-bred terrier who served with the First Battalion Welsh Guards for several years until his retirement in 1980.

with long bodies and short legs, the Dandie Dinmonts were named after a character in a novel by Sir Walter Scott. The last of the Scottish Terriers is another unusual one, with a long flowing coat. This is the **Skye Terrier**, first bred on the island of that name to flush out foxes and badgers from underground. A very keen ratter, the Skye is now a popular show dog, when its full coat is encouraged to grow really long and profuse, and is kept groomed to perfection. Most likely descended from the Skye, with perhaps the addition of some Maltese blood is the diminutive **Yorkshire Terrier**, tiny but full of life and a good ratter.

On the borders between Scotland and England developed the **Bedlington**, which is thought to have close connections with the Dandie Dinmont, but with a degree of Whippet blood which resulted in a tall, fast and very

107

Left: The lovable Yorkshire Terrier puppy grows up to be just as appealing as an adult.

sporting terrier, much easier to train than the more independent breeds. A near neighbour is the small **Border Terrier** with its otter-shaped head and compact body, manufactured to go down fox-holes. Some Border Terriers exported to Canada proved up to tackling any sort of game they encountered, including porcupine, and the breed is favoured by huntsmen for running with Foxhounds. The **Norfolk** and **Norwich Terriers** differ only in their ear set, and are very similar to the Border Terrier. The Norfolk has drop-ears and the Norwich has prick-ears. In the United States of America, both types are still called Norwich Terriers. The breeds were developed for hunting badgers and foxes in East Anglia and were popularized when, because of their diminutive size, they were considered ideal sporting dogs for undergraduates of Cambridge University. The little dogs could be easily concealed within their rooms during studies, and taken out for sport and relaxation in free time and at weekends.

Although called a Terrier, the **Boston** of the United States, really belongs in the Utility Group of dogs. However it was originally bred as a fighting dog and, although it has been modified and refined for the present day show ring, it has remained courageous and is a good little watchdog.

Australia has its own terrier, bred from the Cairn, the Dandie Dinmont and Irish Terriers, combining to produce a compact and fearless dog capable of tackling snakes and any other vermin that comes its way. Only about 10 inches (25 cm) high, it has a blue or silver coat with tan markings, or it may be sandy or red. From the **Australian Terrier** and Yorkshire Terrier came the **Sydney Silkie**, very similar to the Yorkie in type and temperament and equally fearless.

Finally, the **Jack Russell**, though not recognized as a breed, deserves a mention, for it typifies the word terrier for most sportsmen, being tough, tireless and tenacious.

The Boston is not a true terrier, but belongs in the Utility Group of dogs.

Gundogs

The history of today's gundogs stretches back long before the invention of firearms, for dogs with similar tendencies have been prized for centuries for their abilities in finding, flushing and retrieving game. In the 17th century when the sporting gun or 'Fowling Peece' came into use, it allowed greater accuracy and range of kill, but also brought new problems. Muzzle reloading was a slow process, and if game was flushed before the hunter was ready to fire, the shot would be lost. It was not long before 'pointing' and 'setting' dogs were specially bred and trained, first to locate game, then to freeze, standing motionless until the hunter was ready to dispatch it. When breach-loading weapons were invented, it became common practice to drive the quarry towards the guns, and Spaniels came into their own, being ideal for going into any type of undergrowth to flush

out the game. Retrievers quickly became indispensable, too, for running out to collect the shot and wounded trophies. Through the centuries man and dog have worked closely together, in all sorts of weather and over all sorts of terrain, and each of the gundog groups has evolved through careful selection to give us the beautiful and efficient breeds of today.

That Setters were once called English Spaniels is made clear in William Dobson's book *Kunopaedia*, written in 1814. It gives concise instructions for the training of dogs to point and set, but it is headed 'A practical essay on breaking or training the English Spaniel or Pointer, with instructions for attaining the art of shooting flying in which the latter is reduced to rule and the former inculcated on principle'. This is followed by clear instructions showing how to teach a dog to range, point and hunt much as Setters and

Alken's picture shows the newly invented 'fowling pieces' and an eager spaniel waiting to retrieve the fallen waterfowl.

Pointers do today. The art of 'shooting flying' was quite revolutionary, as years after firearms came into common use, birds were still shot as they sat.

The Reverend Daniel in his book *Rural Sports*, published in 1801, wrote, 'In the reign of Charles I, no person shot flying; what is now termed poaching was the gentleman's recreation; and as late as within sixty years an individual who exercised that art was considered as performing something extraordinary and many persons requested to attend his excursions that they might be eye-witnesses of it. Since that period the practice has become more common, and is at present almost universal so that lads of sixteen bring down their birds with all due accuracy.' However shooting flying was mentioned in the British 'Apollo' of 1708, and a poem was penned around 1727, entitled *Ptery-plegia or the art of shooting flying*. In *A History of Riffon* of 1733, the following lines appear:

'His birding-piece the wily Fowler takes
And War upon the feather'd Nation makes.
Whirling the Pheasant mounts, and works his way,
Till Fate flies faster, and commands his stay.'

As guns improved, so gundogs improved and were expected to work in more sophisticated ways. Then, with changes in agricultural methods, driving of game became more and more common. Field trials were conceived and provided good sport, and they have increased in popularity through the years.

Pointers

In Britain during the mid-17th century, the Pointer was used in the hunting field to find and flush out hares for its working partner, the Greyhound, to chase and kill. A picture dated 1725 shows the Duke of Kingston with his kennel of elegant Pointers said to be a blend of Spanish Pointers crossed with the Old French Hounds. At the end of the 18th century, further outcrosses were made with Foxhounds to add bone and stamina to the breed and by the mid-19th century the true **English Pointer** had arrived.

Early setters and pointers seek out game for the guns. National Gallery of British Sports and Pastimes.

The majestic head of the working English Pointer – virtually unchanged for three centuries.

Today the Pointer still works in much the same way as it has done for the past 300 years, first locating game, then indicating the fact by achieving its classical pointing position, nose held high, one foreleg elegantly raised and tail extended out in a line with its back.

The **German Shorthaired Pointer** is also descended from the old Spanish Pointer, and was developed by German sportsmen during the 17th century. As these gentlemen wanted a rather special sort of pointing bird-dog that would also retrieve and trail by night as well as by day, they introduced some Bloodhound for its powers of scent and some Foxhound to add strength and stamina. With the union of the Royal Houses of Hanover and Great Britain in the 19th century, English Pointers were bred with the early German strains and added refinement and elegance to the already efficient breed. Exports were made to the United States and the German Shorthaired Pointer Club was formed there in 1930. Eventually some specimens of the breed made their way to Britain and proved their worth as good all-round gundogs.

Far right: A pair of perfect German Shorthaired Pointers, one showing its natural pointing pose.

The **German Wirehaired Pointer** was evolved from the very best available pointers, and is today a sturdy and adaptable dog for retrieving on land and in water. A feature of the breed is the protective coat, which enables the dog to penetrate the most formidable thorn and bramble.

The **Magyar** or **Hungarian Vizsla** is the national dog of Hungarian sportsmen and is similar in conformation and ability to the German pointing breeds which succeeded it, although drawings made in the time of the Magyar invasions of 1000 years ago, show dogs very like the Vizsla, working in conjunction with falcons, flushing game for the hawks to kill. Another 14th century manuscript also makes it clear that a dog of the Vizsla's characteristics was used in falconry.

Until the First World War Germany had a longhaired pointing dog, evolved from indiscriminate crosses from gundogs of all types, colours and coats, selected for breeding only by virtue of their working ability. By the early 19th century, however, breeders were becoming type-and-colour conscious, and with the foundation of the German Kennel Club, all but the brown-and-white longhaired Pointers were discarded. Any black-and-white puppies born were given away but, being good workers, were often valued by farmers and sportsmen unconcerned with show points. Eventually in 1919 the people of Munster formed a club for their black-and-white dogs, and two years later staged their own show.

Today the **Large Munsterlander** is a good all-round gundog, a keen, steady and admirable retriever. It was introduced to Britain in 1972 and since then it has steadily been gaining in popularity.

In the early 19th century the Dukes of Weimar crossed local Pointers with small Bloodhounds in order to breed a perfect all-round gundog capable of scenting and tracking large animals, as well as hunting small game. Nicknamed the 'grey ghost' because of its distinctive light colouring, the **Weimaraner** Pointer was rarely seen outside its native land until 1929, when Howard Knight managed to purchase a breeding pair to take home with him to the United States of America. Particularly brilliant in working trials and a fine general-purpose hunting dog, the Weimaraner's reputation soon spread and in the 1950s it was imported into Britain.

The Hungarian Vizsla is a large and powerful dog used for all types of field-work.

Left: Spaniels make excellent retrievers from land and water and are particularly easy to train.

Below: Often called 'grey ghosts', Weimaraners also make excellent all-round hunting dogs.

Setters

As early as 1620 Gervase Markham, a contemporary writer of the time, recorded the existence of 'a black and fallow setting dog' in his work on hawking, saying that it was 'the hardest to endure labour'. Then, in 1776, black-and-tan Setters were mentioned again in *A Treatise of Field Diversions*. At the turn of the 19th century, the **Gordon Setter** was a well-established breed, kept in large numbers by the 4th Duke of Richmond and Gordon, at Gordon Castle, Banffshire, Scotland, and had excelled at the first ever field trials at Solihull in 1863, taking the first three prizes.

The Setting Spanyel of 500 years ago had neither the size nor style of today's **English Setter**, but may well have been its main ancestor. However, by the 16th century, two distinct types of bird-dog had evolved. Markham's *The Act of Fowling*, written in 1655, describes the dogs' markings, and they have certainly been passed down to modern times: 'To speak then in a word touching the best choice of this Setting-dogge let him be as neere as you can the best bredde land-spaniell that you can procure: and though some have been curious in observing of their colours, as giving preheminence to the Motley, the Lieur-hude or the white and black spotted.' One of the foremost pioneer breeders of the English Setter was Edward Laverack, who purchased two pure Setters in 1825, and from this foundation produced an excellent strain which survived through a period of 50 years.

Some of the old red-and-white Spaniels of Ireland, bred in turn from the long-legged French Spaniel, are the most probable ancestors of the **Irish Setter**, for even as late as 1874, red-and-white Setters were exhibited in their own classes at the Dublin Show. In the early part of the 19th century the Duke of Enniskillen selectively bred the all-red variety, which were described as being 'blood-red, or rich chestnut or mahogany colour'. Then, in 1876, the Ulster Irish Setter Club decided that the all-red dogs should be called Irish Setters. Today the red-and-white type is rarely seen, but red dogs may be bred with traces of white on the chest, chin or toes, or with a small star or blaze on the face, and these are not classed as disqualifying show faults.

An alert English Setter freezes to mark its game on the moor.

Agility is vital in the gundog and retrievers are taught to return game regardless of obstacles.

Retrievers

Until 1850 or thereabouts, Pointers and Setters were trained to retrieve game. Then it was decided to develop specialized breeds to carry out this task. Existing Setters, Pointers and large Spaniels were used and crossed with dogs brought to Britain by sea-traders, shipping cod from Newfoundland into Poole Harbour, Dorset and other ports along the southern coasts.

A classic work was written by General Hutchinson in 1847. Titled *Dog Breaking* it provides a good record of the Retrievers of this time: 'From education there are good Retrievers of many breeds, but it is usually allowed that as a general rule, the best land

Retrievers are bred from a cross between the Setter and the Newfoundland or the strong Spaniel and the Newfoundland. I do not mean the heavy Labrador whose weight and bulk is valued because it adds to its power of draught, nor the Newfoundland, increased in size at Halifax and St. John's to suit the taste of the English purchaser; but the far slighter dog reared by the settlers on the coast, a dog that is quite as fond of water as of land, and which in almost the severest part of a North American winter will remain on the edge of a rock for hours together watching intently for anything the passing waves may carry near him. Such a dog is highly prized.

A dummy covered with fur or feather is used in training dogs to retrieve.

Without his aid the farmer would secure but few of the many wild ducks he shoots at certain seasons of the year.' The second Earl of Malmesbury lived at Heron Court, near Poole. He bought one of the dogs from Newfoundland and was very impressed with its abilities. In later years his family acquired several more and set up a small breeding kennel. The dog's reputation in the sporting field soon spread across the country and many people became interested in owning such animals. In reply to an enquiring letter from the sixth Duke of Buccleuch in 1887, the third Earl of Malmesbury wrote 'We always call mine Labrador dogs and I have kept the breed as pure as I could from the first I had from Poole, at that time carrying on a brisk trade with Newfoundland. The real breed may be known by having a close coat which turns off the water like oil, and, above all, a tail like an otter.'

In Scotland, other members of the aristocracy had acquired dogs from the Malmesbury imports, and from shipping into the Clyde ports, and eventually the Labrador strains were merged into an homogeneous breed which is the **Labrador Retriever** of today, a fine dependable gundog, guide dog and an excellent sniffer-dog, seeking out drugs and explosives for the police and the army.

Opposite page, top: 'Landseer' Newfoundland dogs coming out of the water.

Opposite page, bottom: A sturdy Chesapeake Bay Retriever in training.

When the Newfoundland and Labrador strains were crossed with the Gordon and Irish Setters a very elegant dog was produced, and called the Wavycoated Retriever. A further outcross and selective breeding reduced the heavy coat which was found to restrict the animal when working in water, and the **Flatcoated Retriever** was born. The breed was very fashionable in the early 1900s and its breed club was formed in 1923. For waterfowling, a special Retriever was bred, its coat consisting of masses of tight curls which insulated the body against the chill of icy water. The **Curly-coated Retriever** like the Flatcoated, is solid black or liver in colour, but the curled coat is thought to have been introduced from the Irish Water Spaniel. Curly-coated Retrievers were a dis-

tinct breed by 1860, and they were shown extensively and exported successfully from Britain to the far corners of the world.

In the year 1807, an English brigantine floundered off the coast of Maryland, and among the survivors, rescued by the American ship *Canton*, were two puppies of Newfoundland type, a red dog and a black bitch. These were presented as gifts to the gentleman who opened his home to the rescued crew, and later, they founded the breed of gundog known as the **Chesapeake Bay Retriever**. This breed excels as a water dog especially in retrieving duck. It has a sedge-coloured coat with natural water-repellant qualities, and is a strong, fearless swimmer with plenty of speed and stamina.

Below: A flatcoated Retriever bitch asking for some exercise.

Popular as a family pet as well as being a superb working dog, the **Golden Retriever** has an interesting history. The first reports of its ancestry told the story of a troupe of performing dogs at a circus in Brighton having been bought by Sir Dudley Majoribanks, later the first Lord Tweedmouth, and used to found the breed – a romantic story but not quite true. Later, a grandson of Lord Tweedmouth explained how his grandfather had seen his first golden dog walking with a man in Brighton. On approaching the man, he learned that he was a cobbler and had been given the dog in lieu of a bad debt, owed to him by the keeper of the Earl of Chichester's kennels. It was considered a throw-out being the only yellow puppy in a litter of black Wavy-coated Retrievers. The next day the dog was purchased by Sir Dudley and was called 'Nous'. Two years later, he was able to buy a Tweed Water-Spaniel bitch named 'Belle', and when the two animals were bred together, their litter of four yellow puppies proved to be the founders of the new breed. The Golden Retriever is highly acclaimed for its work and is a regular competitor at field trials.

Spaniels

Spaniels have a longer history than any other gundog group, and were first used in Spain to drive ground-dwelling birds through the thick cover of their natural habitat, into waiting nets. Even the laws of Hywel Dda, codified in 948, include a mention of the Spaniel, being grouped with the Greyhound as dogs which hunt by sight, in the list of higher kinds of dogs. Many other writers through the centuries refer to these small dogs. The Spaniel was a fashionable dog in the 17th century. Henry II of France was particularly

A successful retrieve by 'Alresford Will Laugh' at field trials.

A shooting party about to set off with their eager Springer Spaniels.

fond of the breed, and the marriage of Charles I to Henrietta Maria of France probably added to its popularity in Britain. Easy to train and economical to keep, the Spaniel type was valued through the ages. In 1667 Nicholas Cox, writing of a small land Spaniel of the time, said, 'You may very well know from a right breed which have been known to be strong, lusty and nimble rangers, of active feet, wanton tails, and busy nostrils, whose tail was without weariness their search without changeableness, and whom no delight did transport beyond fear or 'bedience.'

Thomas Bewick in his *History of Quadrupeds* of 1790 did not differentiate between the Cocker or Springer Spaniels, so it is possible that at that time they were one breed. He wrote 'The Springer or Cocker is lively, active and pleasant, and an unwearied pursuer of its game and very expert in raising woodcocks or snipes from their haunts in woods and marshes.'

The use of the Spaniel in raising woodcock first gave rise to the name of Cocking Spaniel, which in turn became the Cocker. Other Spaniels were used to startle game, so that they sprang up into a net, ran to be coursed by Greyhounds, or rose to be taken by trained hawks. Such dogs were first

called Starters, then Springers. Even as recently as the late 1800s, in the South of England several types of Spaniel could be found in a single litter, the taller puppies being called Springers, the smaller ones Cockers, and any liver-coloured ones called Sussex Spaniels.

The **American Cocker Spaniel** originated in America during the 1870s and was bred from the British Cocker and the American Brown Water Spaniel, a dog popular for working in marshland. The Breed Club was founded in 1881, but the breed today excels best in the show ring. The **Cocker Spaniel** was officially recognized by the Kennel Club in 1892 and the Cocker Spaniel Club was founded in 1902. By the early 1930s, the breed was the most popular dog in Britain, proving itself to be ideal as a family pet as well as an efficient and willing worker.

In 1902 the **English Springer** Spaniel was approved by the Kennel Club and is a substantial little dog, larger than the Cocker, longer in the leg and lighter in the coat. This breed may be of any typical Spaniel colouring, although black-and-white and liver-and-white are preferred. Its smaller, lighter-framed cousin is the **Welsh Springer Spaniel**, originally

called the Welsh name of 'Tarfgi'. This dog is now bred only with a white coat having rich, dark red markings, and was also accepted by the Kennel Club as a separate breed in 1902. Many sportsmen of today consider Springer Spaniels to be the best all-round gundogs in water or on land, and especially for field trial work.

The **Sussex Spaniel** is unique in the fact that it gives tongue when working, and this varies so much in tone and pitch that its owner is said to be able to tell what sort of game has been found. This habit of crying when on the line caused the breed to be penalized in field trials, and many keen competitors replaced their Sussex dogs with other Spaniels resulting in a considerable decline in the breed. In 1859 the writer with the pseudonym 'Stonehenge', an authority on canine matters, penned these words about the Sussex Spaniel: 'He is gifted with a full, bell-like tongue which varies according to the game before him; and by this means an experienced shooter can tell whether to expect fur or feather, and also distinguish a hot scent from a stale one.' Originating nearly 200 years ago, the gloriously golden-coated Sussex Spaniel with its soulful hazel eyes was developed in its pure state for more than 50 years by

The rare and attractive Irish Water Spaniel, close relative of other curled- and corded-coat breeds.

a Mr. W. Fuller who had a kennel near Hastings in the Sussex countryside. At his death in 1847, all but two of the dogs were auctioned off, but this pair was bequeathed to his head keeper, who helped to ensure the continuance of the breed.

Like the stocky Sussex, the **Clumber Spaniel** is a rather slow but steady worker, and ideal for penetrating dense undergrowth to seek out game. Spaniels of this unique breed were first imported into Britain by the second Duke of Newcastle, who had been presented with some breeding stock by the Duc de Noailles of France. A fine portrait entitled 'The Return from Shooting' painted by Francis Wheatley in 1788, shows the Duke seated on his pony and surrounded by friends and dogs including some Clumber Spaniels, believed to have been from the original stock. The name of the breed comes from the Duke's family seat, Clumber Park in Nottinghamshire.

Probably more popular now in some States of America than in Britain, the **Irish Water Spaniel** is used there almost exclusively as a duck dog. The ancestors of the breed were first brought to Ireland by the invading Iberians, later to be known as the Irish Celts. Three sorts of Water Spaniels were known in ancient Ireland, the Northern Spaniel or Old Brown Irish Retriever, the Southern Water Spaniel and the Tweed Water Spaniel. Eventually selective breeding by Mr. Justin McCarthy, who became interested in the dogs in 1829, resulted in the production of a distinctive breed. In 1859 Mr. McCarthy sent this contribution to the sporting magazine, *The Field*: 'I have been the owner of the curly-coated Irish Water Spaniel for the last thirty years and have been, as it were, the godfather of most of those to be disposed of, the dealer always recommending their dogs by saying "they are one of McCarthy's real old breed". I have bestowed many scores of dogs and bitches to gentlemen in every county of Ireland and many parts of England, and bitches have been sent to me from every part of this country for the services of my celebrated dog 'Boatswain', the patriarch of all the highly-bred dogs in this country. There is in reality but two breeds of the true Irish Water Spaniel. In the North the dog has generally short ears without any feather, and is very often of a pied white and brown colour; in the South the dog is of pure liver colour, with long ears and well-curled. . . .

'I have never found them untractable or difficult to train. They readily keep to heel and down charge, and will find a dead or wounded bird anywhere, either in the open or in covert; but they are not partial to stiff thorny brakes as the briars catch in their curls and trail after them. . . . For the gun they should be taught to go into the water like a duck, but when kept for fancy a good dog of this breed will take a flying jump of from twenty-five to thirty-five feet or more, perpendicularly high into the water. My old dog 'Boatswain' lived to about eighteen years old. . . .'

Why Dogs Work

In this book we have tried to show the unique relationship between man and his working dog, which has survived for centuries and is totally unrestricted by boundaries of race, colour, creed or geography. Dogs work willingly for little reward, a word of praise being more than sufficient for their needs. They do this because their innate behavioural patterns elevate their human masters into the position of pack leaders, to be obeyed at all times without question. Man through the ages has observed the natural instincts of dogs, and by selected breeding, and rewarding the slightest desired modification in those instinctive patterns, has produced dogs capable of carrying out all manner of useful tasks. Through this close working relationship, man has formed an emotional and unequalled attachment for the dog which has survived through the ages, and is likely to continue far into the future. Perhaps one of the finest and most perceptive of tributes to a dog was written by Lord Byron following the death of his beloved Newfoundland 'Boatswain'. He wrote:

'Near this spot
Are deposited the remains of one
Who possessed Beauty without Vanity,
Strength without Insolence,
Courage without Ferocity,
And all the virtues of Man
Without his vices.'

Right: Labrador Retrievers like to carry all manners of objects in their soft mouths, a result of generations of careful selective breeding.

Below: A successful retrieve.

Acknowledgments

Fratelli Alinari, Florence 83 top; All Sport: Dave Bunce 72–73, 73 top; Animal Photography – Sally Anne Thompson 20 bottom, 50 right, 80–81, 108–109, 115 top, 118, 118–119, 121 top, 121 bottom; Australian Information Service 23 top, 22–23, 107 top; Barnaby's Picture Library, London 12 bottom, 20 top, 26, 28 bottom, 29 bottom, 56–57, 87, 88, 88–89, 90, 92–93, 93, 95 bottom, 96, 96–97, 102, 106 top, 106 bottom, 112–113, 124, 125; Bibliothèque Nationale, Paris 85; British Museum, London 16–17, 68–69; BPC Picture Library, London 15 top; Bruce Coleman, Uxbridge – Bob & Clara Calhoun 6; Bruce Coleman – Stouffer Prods 12 top; Mary Evans Picture Library, London 24 top, 25 top, 40, 56 bottom, 97 bottom, 98, 99; General Protection Services (Security) Ltd 51 bottom; Photographie Giraudon, Paris 11; Guide Dogs Association 66, 67; Hamlyn Group Picture Library 13 bottom, 16 bottom left, 36–37, 63, 76–77, 82 left, 100, 101, 104–5, 108 left, 109 right, 115 bottom; Mansell Collection, London 14 top, 14 bottom, 34, 35, 38, 70, 71 top, 71 bottom, 82–83, 94, 95 top, 110, 111; Mas, Barcelona 18; Michael Holford, London 13 top, 16 top, 17, 68 left; Robert Hunt, London Library 42 top; Museo del Prado, Madrid 39; Petrovits Laszlo 114; Popperfoto, London 7, 8–9, 10 top, 10 bottom, 22, 30, 32–33, 46 bottom, 48 bottom, 50 left, 53 bottom, 54–55 top, 54–55 bottom, 58, 72, 79, 103, 126; Press Association, London 42–43; Angela Sayer, Crawley 8, 20–21, 24, 28–29, 40–41, 44, 45, 48 top, 49 top left, 49 top right, 49 bottom, 53 top, 52–53, 61, 64 top, 64 bottom, 65, 69 top, 112 left, 116–117, 120, 123; John Topham Picture Library, London 15 bottom, 19, 27, 31, 42 bottom, 46 top, 50–51, 56 top, 59, 60, 62, 84, 86 top, 86 bottom, 91 top, 91 bottom, 107 bottom, 122, 127; Lionel Young 78.

Front cover: John Topham Picture Library, London – John Yates
Back cover: John Topham Picture Library, London – Guy Fleury
Endpapers: Angela Sayer, Crawley
Title spread: Popperfoto, London